# Saving
# Lives with
# Force

## BROOKINGS STUDIES IN FOREIGN POLICY

The Brookings Institution is a private nonprofit organization devoted to research, education, and publication on important issues of domestic and foreign policy. Its principal purpose is to bring knowledge to bear on the major policy problems facing the American people.

On occasion Brookings authors produce relatively short studies that warrant immediate and broad circulation as contributions to public understanding of issues of current national importance. The Brookings Studies in Foreign Policy series is intended to make such studies available to a broad, general audience. In keeping with their purpose, these studies are not subjected to all of the formal review and verification procedures established for the Institution's research publications. As in all Brookings publications, the judgments, conclusions, and recommendations presented in the studies are solely those of the authors and should not be attributed to the trustees, officers, or other staff members of the Institution.

**Studies in Foreign Policy**

# Saving Lives with Force

## Military Criteria for Humanitarian Intervention

MICHAEL O'HANLON

BROOKINGS INSTITUTION PRESS
Washington, D.C.

THE BROOKINGS INSTITUTION
1775 Massachusetts Avenue, N.W., Washington, D.C. 20036

*Library of Congress Cataloging-in-Publication Data*

O'Hanlon, Michael E.
Saving lives with force : military criteria for humanitarian
   intervention / Michael O'Hanlon.
     p. cm.
   Includes bibliographical references and index.
   ISBN 0-8157-6447-2 (pbk.)
    1. Intervention (International law)  2. United Nations—
Armed Forces.  3. Humanitarian assistance, American.  I.
Title.
KZ6369.O38 1997
341.5'84–dc21                                97-21230
                                                  CIP

9 8 7 6 5 4 3 2 1

Typeset in Hiroshige and Copperplate

Composition by Linda Humphrey
Arlington, Virginia

Printed by Kirby Lithographic
Arlington, Virginia

# FOREWORD

International peacekeeping and peace enforcement operations continue to be undertaken by U.S. armed forces—despite the partisan rancor that surrounds debates on multilateral military operations, doubts many Americans harbor toward the United Nations, and the reluctance of the Pentagon to engage in limited military operations in countries of modest direct interest to the United States. Since Desert Storm, the U.S. military has participated in a significant way in such missions in Somalia, Rwanda, Haiti, and Bosnia.

Consequently, it behooves policymakers, military and civilian alike, to think systematically about the conditions under which we should be prepared to participate and how these types of missions can be best conducted.

In this study, Michael O'Hanlon, a defense analyst in the Foreign Policy Studies program, provides a framework for understanding the military dimensions of such operations. Specifically, he analyzes operations likely to be conducted under Chapter VII of the UN Charter to restore order and make possible political reconciliation and reconstruction in countries plagued by violence. He also considers a subset of Chapter VI peacekeeping missions in which one or more parties that originally give their approval to a peace accord and the deployment of outside forces subsequently change their minds and return to violence. In some such cases, outside powers may elect to use peacekeepers to forcibly restore the peace that has been shattered.

Both types of missions often involve combat and pose risks of casualties to outside forces. One of O'Hanlon's principal purposes is to help policymakers foresee the likely determinants of casualties in possible missions in order to better inform choices about when and where to send U.S. troops.

The author would like to extend special thanks to Richard Betts, Richard Haass, Lawrence Korb, Christina Larson, Jack LeCuyer, Tom McNaugher, and Stephen John Stedman. He is also grateful to Roy Alcala, Carl Bradshaw, Francis Deng, Robert Dobson, Harry Dolton, William Durch, John Hillen, Stacey Knobler, Terrence Lyons, Eric Nyberg, Jay Paxton, Yahya Sadowski, Steve Sargeant, James Schear, Stephen Solarz, John Steinbruner, Shibley Telhami, Susan Woodward, and a number of officials of the Department of Defense. Brookings gratefully acknowledges the support of the Carnegie Corporation of New York and the John D. and Catherine T. MacArthur Foundation.

The research was conducted under the supervision of John D. Steinbruner and Richard N. Haass.

The views in this study are those of the author alone and should not be attributed to the trustees, officers, or other staff members of the Brookings Institution.

Summer 1997                                Michael H. Armacost
Washington, D.C.                             President

# Contents

# 1
# INTRODUCTION

A poor understanding of military realities has characterized many recent debates about whether and how to
intervene with force in Bosnia, Rwanda, and
Somalia.[1] Future decisions about using the U.S. military to
assist countries beset by civil violence, usually with these
troops operating as part of a multinational coalition, should be
better informed. Indeed, they must be—for the safety of troops,
the well-being of the populations at risk, and the domestic
political feasibility here in the United States of conducting
future humanitarian interventions.

1. These missions were not complete failures; the operation in Bosnia is providing a reasonable prospect for the peace accord to take hold, and the operation
in Somalia kept alive many tens of thousands of people who would probably not
be otherwise. Still, these missions should have been more effective, and were not
seen as successes by those publics whose support for peace operations and related
interventions is crucial to their political viability. For a discussion of what consti-
tutes success in such missions, see William J. Durch, "Introduction," in William J.
Durch, *The Evolution of U.N. Peacekeeping* (New York: St. Martin's Press, 1993), p.
12; John L. Hirsch and Robert B. Oakley, *Somalia and Operation Restore Hope*
(Washington, D.C.: U.S. Institute of Peace, 1995), p. 150.

However imperfectly past operations of this type have unfolded, and whatever the current views of skeptics about them, recent history and the nature of today's international environment suggest that there will be more in the future. Moral considerations and the U.S. national political ethos will continue to argue for them. As a well-known U.S. Marine general and veteran of recent military operations in Somalia and Iraq put it, "On the Hill, I was challenged a few times about why we ever get involved in this. Well, we get involved with this because we get asked to do it. . . . I'll tell you what— I've walked the ground and seen a lot of dead children. I've seen a lot of people who have starved to death or have been brutally massacred alongside a road. And something inside me says, 'Maybe I shouldn't be doing this, but . . . I *want* to do it.'"[2]

Speaker of the House Newt Gingrich made a broader point, linking the moral issues involved in humanitarian interventions to the credibility of American foreign policy and the broader character of the international community. Discussing policy toward the former Yugoslavia, he argued, "When directly challenged, we must be victorious. The notion of a small band of barbarians directly taking on the civilized democracies and winning is a threat to the entire survival and stability of this planet. And we should respond to it with whatever level of coercion is ultimately required to communicate the fact that we are serious people."[3]

General polling data suggest that the American public thinks very pragmatically about the issue of humanitarian intervention: mitigate suffering where that can be done with high con-

---

2. Lieutenant General Anthony Zinni, U.S. Marine Corps, "It's Not Nice and Neat," *Proceedings*, August 1995, p. 29.

3. See Norman Kempster, "Gingrich Proposes U.S.-Led Bosnia Force," *Los Angeles Times* (Washington ed.), July 19, 1995, p. 3.

fidence, modest cost, and limited duration, but avoid open-ended commitments and high casualties in countries of little direct importance to the United States. Contrary to much of the post-Mogadishu conventional wisdom on the topic, Americans are not opposed to interventions motivated principally by the goal of saving lives, even if there exists some risk of casualties to U.S. soldiers.[4]

Yet a discriminating approach to becoming involved in stopping conflict is absolutely essential. Americans may not fully agree with those realists who argue that peace operations only make sense in defense of major American interests, or with the so-called Weinberger doctrine as it applies to civil conflicts.[5] But they probably do agree with the other criteria that those most wary of intervention demand: concrete objectives, a plausible idea of how the mission will be concluded, a rough estimate of how long it will take, reasonable confidence that its costs in money and mortality will be limited, and good prospects for bringing lasting improvement to the

4. See Steven Kull, "What the Public Knows That Washington Doesn't," *Foreign Policy*, 101 (Winter 1995–96), pp. 102–15. More plausibly, perhaps, but still encouragingly, a recent University of Texas study found that 459 randomly selected participants in a three-day study group, who had initially considered current foreign aid spending too high by a factor of more than 2:1, were evenly split on the matter at the end of their conference.

Americans would seem sympathetic to the logic of Rwanda's current ambassador to the United Nations, Manzi Bakuramutsa, who argued in 1994 that "United Nations peacekeepers go somewhere when there is not much danger. . . . In Rwanda we have films of people begging to be protected in the genocide. And the peacekeepers left." See Barbara Crossette, "When This Rwandan Speaks, the Big Guys Listen," *New York Times*, December 27, 1995, p. A4.

5. As Secretary of Defense Weinberger argued in 1984, "We should only engage *our* troops if we must do so as a matter of our *own* vital national interest. We cannot assume for other sovereign nations the responsibility to defend *their* territory—without their strong invitation—when our own freedom is not threatened." See Caspar W. Weinberger, "The Uses of Military Power," Speech to National Press Club, Washington, D.C., November 28, 1984.

lives of those it is intended to help.[6] As a practical matter a discriminating approach to intervening also seems essential: at least a dozen wars are going on around the world at present, and that number has been about the norm for decades.[7] Some way of prioritizing responses to those conflicts is needed.

In addition, handling such problems is inherently difficult politically, requiring a great deal of time and detailed study from top-level decisionmakers who must understand the peculiarities of a given country if they are to succeed in helping it achieve lasting peace.[8] Critical decisions they must make may include whether to attack extremist factions, to try arresting war criminals, to propose partition of the country at issue, or to ban certain types of ethnically based political parties. To try too many missions is to increase the chances of failure and risk discrediting the very notion of humanitarian intervention among publics whose support is needed.[9]

Washington's decisions about where to participate in selective humanitarian interventions will also be based on factors

6. For a similar set of criteria, see Colin L. Powell, "U.S. Forces: Challenges Ahead," *Foreign Affairs*, vol. 71, no. 5 (Winter 1992–93), p. 38; for others, see Senator John McCain, "The Proper U.S. Role in Peacemaking," in Dennis J. Quinn, *Peace Support Operations and the U.S. Military* (Washington, D.C.: National Defense University Press, 1994), pp. 89–90; and President Clinton's May 1994 directive on peace operations, PDD-25.

7. Those wars are causing casualties at the rate of at least 1,000 deaths per year. International Negotiation Network, *State of World Conflict Report 1994-1995* (Atlanta, Ga.: Carter Center, 1995), pp. 4, 60; Boutros Boutros-Ghali, *An Agenda for Peace* (New York: United Nations, 1992), p. 7.

8. Ambassador James F. Dobbins, "Haiti: A Case Study in Post–Cold War Peacekeeping," Institute for the Study of Diplomacy, Edmund A. Walsh School of Foreign Service, Georgetown University, vol. 2, no. 1, October 1995, p. 5.

9. For a similar viewpoint, see Deputy Assistant Secretary of Defense Sarah Sewall, "Peace Enforcement and the United Nations," in Quinn, *Peace Support Operations*, p. 104.

like a country's proximity to the United States and the degree of linkage between its ethnic groups and key American voting blocs. But these are insufficient decisionmaking criteria for a country with the values of the United States. It is the premise of this study that, where suffering is extreme or threatens to become so, decisions about intervention should also be based on the prospects for relieving that suffering in a relatively low-cost and durable way. The purpose of this study is to help identify the military conditions that tend to make those prospects good.

## THE NEED FOR OUTSIDE MILITARY COMBAT FORCES

Outside powers sometimes have military options short of intervention to address serious violence within a given country. They could use arms transfers, air strikes, blockades, and the like—either to help one side in a civil war win battlefield victory or to exert pressure on an abusive government to change its ways. But those limited tools of military involvement are not always adequate. Too many people may be at imminent risk of death, or general military parity among various factions may appear likely to doom a country to protracted conflict.

If acting from the sidelines of battle is not a viable policy option, what might the international community do instead? Traditionally it has focused on peacekeeping missions in which outside forces deploy after parties to a conflict agree to a cease-fire and provide consent. Those parties, however, often accept mediation and some form of cease-fire only after enduring a protracted military stalemate. This approach carries the risk that much of an entire country will be destroyed in the meantime. In civil wars, the process of getting principal players to peace talks is extremely challenging because it is often not even clear who should be involved in negotiations and what relative influence they should be granted in those negotiations.[10]

Nor does the existence of a cease-fire guarantee that things will go smoothly for peacekeepers. For example, Jonas Savimbi ignored the Angolan peace accord in 1992 after losing the elections the accord had mandated. In Rwanda the August 1993 Arusha peace accord between the Rwandan government and Tutsi-led Rwandan Patriotic Front had already led to the deployment of more than 2,000 peacekeepers before Hutu *genocidaires* destroyed it. The violence that ensued was worse, in human terms, than what had occurred before the peace agreements in the same two countries. International calls for resumption of negotiations and new cease-fires proved powerless to stop the carnage.[11]

Thus outside powers will often not have a choice between diplomacy and the use of force. If the international community wishes to contain or to end a certain conflict rapidly, or at least to mitigate its worst effects on society, it will sometimes need to use major military instruments. And it should expect that at least one party to a conflict is likely to contest its intervention violently.[12]

---

10. I. William Zartmann, "Dynamics and Constraints in Negotiations in Internal Conflicts," in I. William Zartmann, ed., *Elusive Peace: Negotiating an End to Civil Wars* (Brookings, 1995), p. 18; William J. Durch, "Getting Involved: The Political-Military Context," in Durch, *The Evolution of UN Peacekeeping*, pp. 8, 21–22; Fred Charles Ikle, *Every War Must End* (Columbia University Press, 1971), p. 106.

11. See United Nations, *United Nations Peace-Keeping Information Notes, Update: December 1994* (New York, United Nations, 1995), pp. 207–14; Stephen John Stedman, "Consent, Neutrality, and Impartiality in the Tower of Babel and on the Frontlines: United Nations Peacekeeping in the 1990s," in the Disarmament and Conflict Resolution Project's, *Managing Arms in Peace Processes: The Issues* (United Nations, 1996), pp. 35–56; personal communication from Stephen Stedman.

12. For similar views, see Durch, "Getting Involved," p. 25; Richard K. Betts, "The Delusion of Impartial Intervention," *Foreign Affairs*, vol. 73, no. 6 (November/December 1994), pp. 20–33; and Stephen John Stedman, "Alchemy for a New World Order," *Foreign Affairs*, vol. 74, no. 3 (May/June 1995), pp. 17–18.

The international community could sometimes obtain leverage over local parties, or relief for a given persecuted group, by creating a safe haven within or adjacent to the country at issue.[13] But such partial solutions are most promising for conflicts such as wars of secession, in which a clear victim people can be identified not only by race or religion but by geographic location. When there is a general breakdown of order or a murderous regime, many civilians throughout a country are likely to be at acute risk. In such a case it may be necessary effectively to make much of the country a safe haven. In other words, it may be necessary to invade, establish control, and temporarily play the role of sovereign over much or all of a country's territory. If what Stephen Stedman calls "spoilers" back out of a peace accord and resort to violence, it may also be necessary to expand the scope of a peacekeeping operation to take on more muscular attributes.

A military operation with these goals might be termed a peace enforcement operation or peace imposition.[14] But it is probably better to leave the modifier "peace" entirely out of the terminology and describe it as intervention to restore order. To convey a sense of its humanitarian benefits and emphasize that it is not a war of conquest, outside powers might describe the operation with concepts of just war theory, in which great importance attaches to preventing noncombatant casualties. They should also emphasize that the goal of their operation is to respect the principle of sovereignty by

13. For a concurring opinion, see Richard N. Haass, *Intervention: The Use of American Military Force in the Post–Cold War World* (Washington, D.C.: Carnegie Endowment, 1994), pp. 87–100.

14. For a good description of many of the different types of peace-related operations now being used or contemplated, see Headquarters, Department of the Army, *FM 100-23: Peace Operations* (December 1994), pp. 2–15; see also Boutros-Ghali, *An Agenda for Peace;* and Executive Office of the President, "The Clinton Administration's Policy on Reforming Multilateral Peace Operations," May 1994, p. 12.

quickly restoring rule to a representative, or at least fair and indigenous, government.[15]

In any humanitarian operation, there is a natural tradeoff between intervening early and intervening late. If peacekeepers are deployed to support a peace accord that subsequently falls apart, there is also a tension between, on the one hand, quickly using force against violators of the accord and, on the other, trying to cajole them back into voluntary compliance.

Conventional wisdom holds that the use of force should be a last resort, used only after diplomacy and other measures have been attempted and found wanting.

At the same time, it is highly desirable to intervene as soon as possible in a conflict that seems destined to be severe. The humanitarian benefits of doing so are often obvious. In addition, though it is sometimes said that civil wars must burn themselves out before peace is possible, they can accelerate as easily as they can reach some natural exhaustion point. The bitterness war engenders, and its tendency to enhance the power and influence of destructive leaders and groups while weakening or eliminating constructive forces in society, can add to the momentum of war for a substantial period of time before the war and the hatred begin to recede.[16] Even when wars do finally seem to burn themselves out, it is often only after many, many years.

Deciding to intervene early is difficult. Doing so depends on reaching a rapid judgment about whether or not a conflict has "bad guys" and "good guys," figuring out which are which, and

15. See for example, Michael Walzer, *Just and Unjust Wars* (New York: Basic Books, 1977), pp. 101–08; Francis M. Deng and others, *Sovereignty as Responsibility* (Washington, D.C.: Brookings, 1996).

16. Terrence Lyons and Ahmed I. Samatar, *Somalia: State Collapse, Multilateral Intervention, and Strategies for Political Reconstruction* (Brookings, 1995), p. 31; Michael S. Lund, *Preventing Violent Conflicts* (Washington, D.C.: U.S. Institute of Peace, 1996), pp. 14–15.

formulating an intervention strategy accordingly. Reaching the wrong decision can be disastrous. For example, an external intervention in Zaire's refugee crisis of late 1996 that sought simply to impose a cease-fire and allow refugees to be fed might have done more harm than good. Had it prevented the local and largely Tutsi "banyamulenge" from driving Hutu extremists out of the camps, it would have perpetuated a problem that was in fact later solved by the unfettered actions of regional participants to the conflict. But policymakers should not shrink from difficult decisions on the pretext that they must give all nonmilitary instruments of policy their due. In the Uganda of Idi Amin or the Rwanda of the Hutu-extremist interahamwe, for example, decisive and early response to violence by outside forces would have been fully justified—and highly desirable.

## Summary

This study attempts to identify the salient military questions that policymakers considering intervention should scrutinize and to provide a framework for investigating them in specific cases.

### Military Mechanics

Chapter 2 is primarily a chronological description of how intervening forces would deploy and set out to establish control of a country, including possible use of tactical combat operations to neutralize extremist armed groups or to rescue a failed peacekeeping mission that had originally been deployed with the consent of indigenous parties. The chapter is similar in scope to a Department of Defense field manual, focusing on military technicalities, but it considers a type of operation somewhere between infantry combat and peace operations (topics on which the U.S. Army has already written useful guides). It is intended largely as background for the calculations of chapter 4. But it also demonstrates that the conduct of this type of operation can be fairly specifically planned. It shows that one can be confident about successfully completing its basic military steps—provided that a top-notch western military, and preferably that of the United States, provides significant assets, including strategic and tactical airlift and combat forces.

*Policy*

The third chapter considers broader matters of policy, reflecting on the pros and cons of various types of mandates and exit strategies and establishing the link between them and a mission's likely duration.

Exit strategies are critical. Any humanitarian intervention of the type considered here is much more than a military deployment (unless outside forces simply choose to help one side win a war or provide general security to relieve acute suffering and then depart without improving the basic security landscape of a country). Notably, indigenous governments and security forces generally will need to be rebuilt or allowed to rebuild themselves. Which domestic players participate in such processes and which do not will significantly alter the country's future prospects. So, clearly, will decisions about whether or not to countenance partition of a country.

Given the sensitivities that most policymakers have about nation-building (or, more accurately, "state-building") activities in the light of experience in Vietnam, Lebanon, and Somalia, it is hardly necessary to elaborate on the dangers associated with trying to help restore governments and security institutions.[17] Yet it is equally important not to dismiss such efforts. After all,

---

17. My thanks to Stephan Stedman for emphasizing the distinction between nation building and state building.

the international community has of late been undertaking numerous activities like holding elections, improving police and security forces, and assisting economic reconstruction in the wake of civil wars. The question is not whether to try in the abstract, but what can be done in a specific case.

## Costs

The final chapter focuses on other questions likely to be of greatest concern to policymakers and also subject to numerical estimates (albeit very approximate ones): the likely budgetary costs of any operation and the likely human costs to interveners. The financial costs are fairly predictable on a day-to-day and month-to-month basis, and already rather familiar to those who have followed recent operations in places such as Panama, Somalia, and Bosnia: generally one to several billion dollars a year in marginal expenditures. That range covers most operations of interest, generally requiring roughly 20,000 to 60,000 uniformed personnel. Forces of that size are appropriate for interventions in most small to medium-size countries, assuming potentially hostile forces numbering in the thousands or low tens of thousands.

## Conclusions

Five other conclusions follow from the analysis. First, intervention to restore order in a relatively small country is generally feasible. That was demonstrated vividly by the U.S. military operation in Panama (though not all future missions would necessarily go so smoothly, given the U.S. military's unusual access to parts of Panama before the operation to overthrow President Mañuel Noriega). However, transport and logistics capabilities are at a premium, and rapid maneuver is very important. For these reasons, U.S. military participation is generally a prerequisite to success, though the French and British may be able to handle the lead role in smaller operations. Also, armed units of the traditional sort, rather than designated peacekeeping forces, appear the right ones to take on these logistically challenging and militarily dangerous tasks.

Second, deaths and other casualties to intervening forces are likely. The total number might be small (as in the case of the U.S. invasion of Haiti in 1994) but would more commonly reach into the dozens or low hundreds (as in Panama and Somalia). The total could reach the high hundreds if the country in which the troops were intervening had reasonably well-equipped armies, difficult terrain, or dedicated fighters; should all of those circumstances coincide, casualties to intervening forces could exceed 1,000 (with about 15 to 20 percent of the total number of casualties being deaths).

Third, there is virtually nothing of a military nature that outside forces can do to prevent the possibility of protracted guerrilla resistance against their intervention. Even if the initial phases of seizing key infrastructure and establishing general order are accomplished promptly and at modest cost, as is likely in most countries of interest, sustained resistance is entirely possible thereafter. It could lead to several times as many deaths among intervening soldiers as would be incurred during the initial phases of the intervention. This finding means that operations to "keep the peace" can be almost as dangerous as operations to "make a peace." In other words, if local parties consent to the deployment of peacekeepers, but then turn against them and against a peace accord that had been previously signed, the peacekeeping mission could become quite bloody. It is worth remembering that the Rwandan genocide occurred after a peace agreement had been signed and peacekeepers deployed; if those peacekeepers had simply enforced the accord to which principal parties had already committed themselves, their mission would have been very dangerous (and indeed, as things turned out, ten peace-keepers lost their lives before the mission could be terminated).

Fourth, the odds of concerted indigenous resistance hinge largely on the politics of the country at issue—and an informed judgment about those politics should therefore be part of any decision to intervene. In some cases, interveners will by their simple presence and capabilities intimidate virtually all possible opposition and be able easily to establish order and help rekindle reconstruction. In others, they will be tested by factions or leaders with little interest in a democratic process and a considerable willingness to suffer casualties in order to drive interveners out of their country. Sometimes it will be difficult or impossible to ascertain in advance which set of conditions applies, and policymakers will act on the basis of misperceptions. Humanitarian interventions will not, therefore, always go according to plan.

Fifth and finally, the likelihood of dedicated resistance is often also a sensitive function of how an intervention is conducted and what its goals are. For example, policymakers may elect to have outside armed forces attack and weaken an extremist indigenous group in a given country. Or they may choose a strategy of trying to "live and let live"—focusing their energies on building up the country's domestic security institutions in the hope that those institutions will someday be able to contain extremists on their own. The decision they make could greatly affect their own casualty rate and the overall prospects for the country's long-term recovery from war.

Sometimes risking more casualties to intervening forces may improve the long-term prospects for peace, but in other cases it may not. To take another type of example, allowing an extremist faction or ethnic group to secede from a country may limit risks to intervening forces and also improve the chances for lasting peace in the region.

A number of these points can be illustrated by reference to the world's interventions in Somalia in 1992–93 and in Bosnia in the early to mid-1990s. Many mistakes were made in the Somalia intervention, but most of them were political rather than military. National military leaders deserve part of the responsibility for the mission's shortcomings since they knew at least as much about the overall political-military situation in Somalia as anyone else and were involved in crucial decisions such as whether to pursue the notorious warlord General Mohammed Aideed. But leaders and troops on the ground performed very competently. It is difficult to imagine better tactics or other improvements that would have ensured a more favorable outcome. Though helicopters might have been operated differently in any subsequent missions, given their unexpected vulnerability to Somali rocket-propelled grenades as evidenced on October 3, 1993, they would not have been effective if kept at too great a distance. Other vulnerabilities of the force would have persisted as well.

The militaries of the United States and other countries established control of key facilities, maintained proper patrols, and set up fairly good human intelligence networks (though they were sometimes penetrated by Aideed's partisans). With the notable exception of the slaying of twenty-four Pakistani peacekeepers in June of 1993, they also prevailed decisively in most firefights. They seriously weakened General Aideed's forces in the fateful fight of October 1993 in which eighteen U.S. servicemen also lost their lives. They could probably have significantly diminished his faction's strength vis-à-vis the others in Somalia had they been willing to engage Aideed's forces again and sustain comparable numbers of casualties over the next few weeks. Doing so might have given other factions an opportunity to form a coalition government and unified security forces.

Pursuing Aideed would have been a perfectly sound policy had the risks been recognized and President Clinton been prepared to rally public and congressional support for the operation despite those risks. Intervening simply to ease the humanitarian catastrophe and then withdraw would also have been an acceptable and internally consistent policy. What was unacceptable was trying to pursue Aideed while giving the public and its representatives on Capitol Hill the impression that the risks were no greater than those that might have been expected in simply easing the humanitarian disaster.

The case of Bosnia illustrates the importance of choosing a mission mandate that is consistent with the political-military realities of a given country. Early calls for intervention there to defeat Serb forces and reimpose a unified Bosnian state under the Muslim-led government might well have incited dedicated guerrilla resistance by the Serbs. But operations to drive Serb forces from specific tracts of land were possible at limited cost (at least late in the war), as combined Croat-Muslim forces demonstrated in late 1995. Also, the earlier use of air strikes to destroy artillery being used in ethnic cleansing operations or the siege of Sarajevo could probably have helped protect populations and facilitate peace talks—just as it ultimately did in the months before Dayton.

In the aftermath of the Dayton accords, keeping the peace has proven relatively safe in the IFOR (implementation force) and SFOR (stabilization force) operations. But using troops from NATO states and other countries to pursue war criminals and forcibly resettle refugees would be considerably riskier. For that reason, it has been wise not to use them for such purposes on a large scale, especially against the most heavily protected suspects, like Ratko Mladic and Radovan Karadzic. Directly opposing ethnic cleansing and genocide in Bosnia when they were occurring would have been a defensible policy. Using limited force to help along a peace process and then using outside forces to keep the peace has been a constructive and tenable policy as well. But choosing to escalate a low-risk peacekeeping mission into a dangerous military operation risks quickly losing the support of the American public—just as happened in Somalia.

Given the inadvisability of those operations, the lack of meaningful progress toward reintegration of the three Bosnian entities into a single state, the continued existence of three largely hostile armed forces within the country's territory, and the international community's mounting desire to leave Bosnia soon, another conclusion also seems inescapable. It is time to call a spade a spade and allow Bosnia to be divided into three separate entities. Doing so soon, while outside forces are still in the country, will allow tempers to cool and access agreements over disputed regions like the Brcko corridor to be worked out before the Bosnians are again on their own. Umbrella organizations governing not only transit routes and shared infrastructure but economic cooperation, protection of minority rights, and other matters of shared concern are needed within Bosnia, to be sure. But they should not be confused with a single national government.

These examples underscore both the potential and the limitations of forcible intervention. They should help brace policymakers for the types of risks that could be involved in future operations—and convince them of the need to make explicit decisions about tradeoffs as well as to lobby their publics to support whatever mission mandate and exit strategy are adopted.

Finally, policymakers and the general public should bear in mind that there do not appear to be any straightforward modifications to military technology, strategy, or tactics that can make such operations substantially less risky. At the same time, if the emergence of a snowballing guerrilla resistance movement is unlikely and if outside parties are willing to pay a modest blood price in any intervention—two very big ifs—they will generally be able to help give local populations an opportunity to reconstruct their countries in peace.

# 2
# PLANNING AND CONDUCTING
# AN INTERVENTION

---

**W**hat operations would intervening forces have to conduct to establish themselves in a violence-ridden country, ensure their own security, and then restore stability and order for the country's population? If they were deployed into a country with a tenuous cease-fire and enjoyed the initial consent of indigenous parties, but later saw that cease-fire collapse and violence resume, what steps would they need to take to restore the cease-fire?

The answers to these questions are fairly straightforward for the U.S. military or a multinational force with strong U.S. representation. Requirements are not trivial, and the steps needed in any mission are somewhat complex and time consuming. But the tasks can be clearly specified in technical military terms, even if they are not without danger to the troops carrying them out. With a few exceptions like airlift, special forces, and military police, most U.S. capabilities would not be heavily taxed by such an operation.

Establishing control of a country requires three main steps, not necessarily entirely discrete and sequential. Indeed, the

U.S. military would prefer that they largely coincide when possible, as in the 1989 invasion of Panama, to achieve overwhelming and rapid dominance of the situation. In perhaps the most likely case, the stages would each begin at distinct moments but end up overlapping. For cases in which a cease-fire collapsed after peacekeepers had been deployed, only the third stage would typically be of major military concern.

First, intervening forces would have to get into the country, establish lodgments, and ensure their self-defense capabilities. They would also have to seize major facilities and population centers in order to establish overall control of the territory. Finally, they would tactically pursue any indigenous forces that refused to cooperate with the cease-fire they were seeking to impose, while at the same time extending security to the country's smaller cities and towns as resources permitted. This latter step might not be the last one to begin: intervening forces might be obliged to commence it as they arrive, if they immediately encounter concerted resistance.

In cases where a cease-fire or peace accord was in place when peacekeepers arrived but later collapsed, as in Angola in 1992 and Rwanda in 1994, this last step would be the only one carried out in the face of resistance. But if peacekeepers were deployed to countries with particularly delicate peace accords, they would be wise to expect opposition as they started operations and to take precautions accordingly. Thus some dimensions of the first two stages of the operation described in this chapter could still be germane. Specifically, peacekeepers should generally deploy and conduct operations in sufficient strength to defend themselves if necessary.

One point deserves special emphasis: because indigenous militias will not always be clearly identifiable and stationary, intervening forces will often not be able to simply "separate" them from each other, as proponents of peace enforcement operations often suggest. Those factions may not have any interest in being separated. They may disperse or relocate at least their light weaponry—the vast majority of the armaments in most civil conflicts—if engaged or screened. Their natural tendency will often be to behave like guerrilla units if faced by an overwhelmingly more powerful outside force.

The second principal challenge to the ultimate success of this type of mission is the difficulty of reforming indigenous police and army forces so they can ensure order after the interveners depart. Doing so would often require purging some existing personnel and giving some former rebels the opportunity to join official police or army ranks. This task is not easy to accomplish. But even if it smacks of nation-building, it is critical, and a mission should generally not be attempted without some assessment of how feasible it would be.

## Establishing Lodgments

An intervening force might well encounter some resistance as it began to deploy into the country in question. Even in the event that widespread anarchy prevailed, some indigenous groups—perhaps the most radical or best armed of the lot—might see the end of conflict and an attempt to effect political reconstruction as antithetical to their aims and thus view the interveners as the enemy. If those groups controlled the country's critical points of entry and did not support the arrival of outside forces, they could make life difficult.

As a rule combat troops should be the first to deploy into the country in question. As in any deployment into a combat zone, they should immediately set out to establish site security at the ports or airfields of debarkation.[1] Those sites need to be made

---

1. Headquarters, Department of the Army, *Field Manual 100-5: Operations* (Washington, D.C.: 1993), pp. 3–4 through 3–5.

defensible from all directions against direct-fire weapons—tanks, rifles, antiair weapons, and the like—necessitating an area of control several kilometers in width. The deploying unit should be deployed as an integral whole and should be put in place in the shortest amount of time possible to minimize its vulnerability during this sensitive arrival phase. If indigenous forces possessed substantial antiair artillery or surface-to-air missiles or even rocket-propelled grenades, the first arriving forces might need to deploy in the general vicinity of an objective by parachute (one brigade of the 82d Airborne Division is generally on alert at any time and could be used if the need for such a mission developed). They should then fight or maneuver their way to the airfield and secure it as well as the surrounding area so that subsequent arrivals could land directly on runways.[2]

The intervening force should probably deploy at least a brigade at any point of entry. A brigade of force (roughly 3,000 to 5,000 troops) provides a wide range of critical capabilities in a modern military, including headquarters capable of interacting with national command authorities, construction and engineering units, aviation and artillery battalions, and standard infantry or armored combat units. In a large country or a country with several major population centers, brigade-sized forces would probably need to be deployed at more than one site.

A division is even more self-sufficient than a brigade for support such as medical and logistics units. It also possesses air defense, helicopter, intelligence, and greater integrated communications capabilities. Generally, therefore, an intervention operation should be at least division-strong countrywide.

---

2. Congressional Budget Office, "Options for Strategic Airlift" (October 1995), p. 10; Headquarters, Department of the Army, FM 100-5: Operations, p. 3-10; Commandant, U.S. Army Infantry School, "The Application of Peace Enforcement Operations at Brigade and Battalion," Fort Benning, Georgia, August, 1994, p. 9.

Moreover, a division is led by a two-star general and thus has greater prestige than a colonel-led brigade.[3]

## Deploying the Forces

Deploying a light brigade can be done with a single flight of roughly half of the U.S. airlift fleet—that is, with 200 to 300 C-141 aircraft or the equivalent.[4] If forces must deploy by parachute for reasons indicated above, only the C-141 and C-17 aircraft would be usable, in which case an intervening force—assumed to have the U.S. airlift fleet available to it—could only deploy a brigade at a time (C-5s as well as the civil reserve air fleet could not be used for these purposes).

If a nearby country could provide a staging base, however, C-130 aircraft could also be used to shuttle in troops much more quickly. The operation might take a few days to prepare, since forces would need to be predeployed into that third country before setting out to establish their lodgment. For a spot 10,000 kilometers away from the United States, it would take a typical aircraft about three days to make a complete round trip, including loading and unloading and minimal maintenance. Using a sizable fraction of the 500 C-130 aircraft in the U.S. military's air fleet would add the equivalent of another 200 C-141s. The United States might thus have the ability to deploy up to three brigades into the violence-ridden country in a single sortie—and perhaps conduct two or even three sorties per day.

Inevitably, the actual performance of airlift tends to be less than its theoretical capacity. Runways and unloading facilities, as

3. *Field Manual 100-5*, p. 8-4; Headquarters, Department of the Army, *Organization of the United States Army* (Washington, D.C.: June 1994), pp. J-6 through J-7.

4. The fleet totals about 700 C-141 equivalents at present, of which roughly two-thirds is military-owned and the rest part of the civilian reserve airlift fleet. See Congressional Budget Office, *Improving Strategic Mobility: The C-17 Program and Alternatives* (September 1986), pp. 44–49; Secretary of Defense William J. Perry, *Annual Report to the President and the Congress* (February 1995), pp. 218–25.

well as the availability of fuel and the infrastructure to dispense it, could limit the throughput at any given airfield. Even the best-equipped Saudi bases handled no more than seventy flights a day during Desert Shield and Storm. (One wonders, given the fact that major commercial airports handle that number of flights per hour, if this number could be augmented substantially with a better approach to air traffic control and infrastructural improvements. But those improvements may not be possible in the types of austere conditions likely to be found in the settings considered here.)[5] Still, it seems likely that sufficient airfields would be available to deploy several brigades of light forces and their support elements within about a week. Even smaller and poorer countries in places such as Africa and Central America tend to have several airfields capable of handling U.S. strategic lift aircraft.[6]

As noted, an airlift fleet comparable in size to that of the U.S. military would be needed to achieve such a deployment rate. It would only be available if the United States was willing to forgo any other airlift requirements during that time.[7] In the latter event, airborne assault would usually not be possible.

5. Congressional Budget Office, "Planning for Defense: Affordability and Capability of the Administration's Program" (March 1994), pp. 27–28 and 39–40; Christopher Bowie and others, *The New Calculus: Analyzing Airpower's Changing Role in Joint Theater Campaigns* (Santa Monica, Calif.: RAND Corporation, 1993) p. 35; U.S. Air Force, *Gulf War Air Power Survey*, vol. 3, *Logistics and Support* (Washington, D.C.: Government Printing Office, 1993), p. 101; Congressional Budget Office, "Options for Strategic Airlift," October, 1995, pp. 3–6.

6. General Accounting Office, *Military Airlift: Comparison of C-5 and C-17 Airfield Availability*, GAO-NSIAD-94-225 (July 1994), pp. 12–13.

7. The major European militaries have typically only a few tens of medium-range transport each. Their commercial airline industries typically each have about fifty aircraft with ranges of 10,000 kilometers or more and capacities of 250 passengers or more. However, using these aircraft for military missions would presumably be difficult in any but the most dire of national emergencies and could not suffice to transport significant amounts of the equipment that even light forces require. Thus European capabilities are limited. See International Institute for Strategic Studies, *The Military Balance 1995–1996* (Oxford, England: Oxford University Press, 1995); *World Aviation Directory* (New York: McGraw Hill, 1994).

Particularly for missions in landlocked countries, it would be desirable for several neighboring states to provide overflight rights. Without such rights, the operation might prove impossible—unless the United States and other countries chose simply to seize overflight privileges.

In the unlikely event that significant amounts of heavy weaponry were needed for an operation, sealift would be needed, and for that reason the ability to deploy forces within days would be lost. A U.S. light division of some 10,000 troops might be airlifted in 400 C-141 sorties, and an airborne division in about 800. But a heavy division—weighing 200,000 tons, or ten times as much as a light division, and including more than 1,000 pieces of large combat equipment as well as even more trucks and other large vehicles—would require around 5,000 sorties, corresponding to several weeks of continuous operations by the entire U.S. airlift fleet. Support and supplies for just thirty days of combat-like operations would be again as heavy.[8]

At most, therefore, one might consider deploying and sustaining a heavy brigade by air. Establishing military dominance in a country where more heavy forces would be required—or even sustaining a large infantry force over time—would require some type of access to the sea, either directly or via major road or rail network.

To deploy forces by sea, several weeks are needed. Even fast sealift ships, traveling at thirty knots and thus covering more than 1,000 kilometers a day once embarked, would generally require at least fifteen to twenty days to get equipment to a given country from the United States. Vulnerable port infrastructure must be protected in the country of destination in the meantime or rebuilt when forces arrive if it has been damaged

8. Congressional Budget Office, *Rapid Deployment Forces: Policy and Budgetary Implications* (February 1983), p. 29.

by warfare. The United States has enough such ships to deploy a heavy division at a time, if their availability for immediate response to other possible scenarios such as a major regional war can be forgone. It also has Marine equipment stored on ships in brigade quantities near Southwest Asia and Northeast Asia, and a heavy brigade's worth of Army equipment afloat in the Indian Ocean region. Finally, it has the Marine Corps amphibious fleet (actually operated by the Navy), with a combined carrying capacity of nearly one division. Thus it could in theory deploy more than two divisions of equipment to most parts of the world within several weeks.[9]

No other country in the world has any capacity of note within such a time frame. Thus, unless the conflict-ridden country at issue was adjacent to a major European or Asian power, any heavy response within the first month would be predominantly American.[10]

Fortunately, only modest numbers of heavy forces would generally be needed for forcible humanitarian intervention. Even in the more difficult cases, such as Somalia, the forces controlled by local factions are usually light in nature. Weaponry is often plentiful, and some heavy weaponry in the form of mortars and artillery can be found, but no significant heavy combined-arms forces operate. The Bosnia conflict, though itself primarily a war of light weapons and some artillery, was on the upper end of the heaviness scale that might be expected. So most civil wars of the type at issue could probably be handled without seaborne deployment of combat forces—though they would, as noted, usually require ships for sustainment and for humanitarian efforts.

9. Navy League of the United States, *The Almanac of Seapower 1994* (January 1994), pp. 168–69; Congressional Budget Office, "Options for Strategic Airlift" (October 1995), p. 2.

10. John E. Peters and Howard Deshong, *Out of Area or Out of Reach?: European Military Support for Operations in Southwest Asia* (Santa Monica, Calif.: RAND Corporation, 1995), p. 92.

If fast sealift ships and maritime prepositioned stocks and the like were unavailable, it might take two to three months to deploy substantial heavy forces. (It would also take at least two months to put a heavy force consisting of much more than two U.S. divisions in place.)[11]

## Establishing Strongholds

Once safely deployed, how would an intervening force establish a nationwide presence in key areas where it could protect most of the population and infrastructure in the country at issue? In the event that options were available to it, a deploying force would probably have made its decisions about where to arrive not only on the basis of where arrival was easiest but of where it allowed for the quickest and safest establishment of general presence in the next phase of the military operation. Thus forces might have deployed into the capital city region even if resistance there was somewhat greater or terrain somewhat less favorable than in other parts of the country. They might instead, as suggested above, have deployed directly into several cities or regions if doing so allowed for a more timely establishment of order throughout the country than landing at a single place. Either way, what would come next?

The specific types of strongholds to be established are fairly similar from country to country. They include major population centers; major nodes of economic activity; and the machinery of political control such as military and police installations, prisons and courts, central banks, media channels, and the basic infrastructure of government.

The major economic assets would include as top priorities any infrastructure that would be very costly to repair or especially

---

11. Secretary of Defense William J. Perry, *Annual Report to the President and the Congress* (February 1995), pp. 35, 224.

hazardous to lose to forces that might resort to terrorism—facilities such as major oil production and refining capabilities, power plants, dams, water pumping and purification stations, chemical factories, nuclear reactors, telephone switching stations, granaries, perhaps some large buildings, and major bridges.

Major population centers would include first and foremost large cities, and most countries germane to this study might have several. Thereafter, security would also be established at chief regional centers. Securing such centers and perhaps some neighboring territory suitable for temporarily housing any internally displaced persons would also provide a network of safe havens in case ongoing lower-level conflict in the country-side took some time to quell.[12] Finally, in countries where warlords dominated a major city—as with Aideed and his competitors in Mogadishu, Somalia—expanding the mission quickly to several regions would have political advantages. It would allow outside forces quickly to involve a broader set of domestic players as they sought to catalyze formation of a new government; it would also provide their operation with as much political legitimacy and cover as possible.

To protect a country's economic infrastructure and most of its population, a rough rule of thumb might be that an intervening force should rapidly establish a substantial presence in cities with more than 100,000 people. There are typically ten or more such cities in mid-sized developing countries.

### Specific Examples

It is difficult to proceed further in this discussion in the abstract; a couple of examples may help. Iraq is a convenient

12. For an argument that, in some cases, establishing such safe havens might even be the wisest ultimate goal for an outside effort to relieve suffering, see Richard N. Haass, *Intervention: The Use of American Military Force in the Post-Cold War World* (Washington, D.C.: Carnegie Endowment, 1995), pp. 97–100.

case because of the plethora of Gulf War data. It is perhaps somewhat wealthier than the typical country experiencing a general breakdown of order and security. But it is typical in geographic size—about half a million square kilometers, slightly smaller than Afghanistan and Somalia, twice the size of the former Yugoslavia, three times the size of Cambodia, four times the size of Liberia, and twenty times the size of Haiti and Rwanda. It also presents a representative variability of terrain, including seacoast, marsh, plains, and mountains. Its population of nearly 20 million is within the range of 3 million to 25 million for the above-mentioned countries. How many facilities that might be termed key assets, and how many large cities and towns, does Iraq have?

To answer the first question, consider Gulf War targets. U.S. planners focused on roughly 200 targets, about evenly divided between military and nonmilitary assets. A later Air Force document confirmed that such a target set was illustrative of what might be found in other medium-sized countries that could be of military concern to the United States in the future.[13] Of the nonmilitary assets, oil and electricity facilities, key railroad nodes, and airfields each accounted for about twenty-five targets. In the military category, about half the sites were depots and other major materiel sites; the others were command and control and air defense facilities, as well as sites suspected of involvement in the production or stockpiling of unconventional weapons.[14]

Not all of these sites would be of equal importance in an

13. Department of the Air Force, "The Bomber Roadmap" (June 1992), p. 4.

14. Thomas A. Keaney and Eliot A. Cohen, *Gulf War Air Power Survey Summary Report* (Government Printing Office, 1993), p. 42. In more advanced economies, there might also be several tens of major facilities associated with production of metals and the like; see Frederic S. Nyland, "Exemplary Industrial Targets for Controlled Conflict," in Desmond Ball and Jeffrey Richelson, eds., *Strategic Nuclear Targeting* (Cornell University Press, 1986), p. 215.

effort to restore order. In addition, some would probably be located near each other, allowing one unit to protect more than one of them. Thus for a country the size of Iraq, perhaps only 100 sites might be of acute concern. Such a country would also include about ten to twenty small cities of more than 100,000 individuals and one or two major metropolitan areas of more than 1,000,000 people.[15]

What size force does the defense of each key site require? Although the nature of indigenous threats clearly must be weighed, it is generally considered appropriate to use brigade-sized forces to defend critical sites against the possibility of concentrated and sustained attack. For smaller sites, or those less vulnerable to attack, a battalion—with roughly one-third to one-fifth the strength of a brigade—may suffice. Battalions are administratively self-sufficient and capable of some independent operations of the type that might be needed to repulse an attack against the assets they are charged to defend.

If neighboring sites were close enough, a battalion's companies might each defend an individual site, supporting each other if put under attack so that the battalion overall could cover several. This approach would begin to stretch forces thin in many situations, but it might be feasible in others.[16] Battalions would also usually be the minimum acceptable unit for ensuring security throughout an urban area. Larger cities would generally require at least a brigade.

Forces of such a size also would seem to be adequate when taking into account the experience of military patrols along

15. Central Intelligence Agency, *The World Factbook 1995–1996* (Washington, D.C.: Brassey's, 1995); Brian Hunter, ed., *The Statesman's Yearbook 1995–1996* (New York: St. Martin's, 1995).

16. Headquarters, U.S. Army, *Organization of the United States Army* (June 1994), p. J-2 through J-6. Moving down the organizational hierarchy of the U.S. Army, battalions and companies have about 300 to 1,000, and 60 to 200 troops, respectively.

demilitarized zones. Generally, using the Sinai and Golan Heights and Cyprus as benchmarks, every kilometer of cease-fire or separation line requires ten to twenty peacekeepers to survey it. A city of several kilometers diameter (ten to twenty square kilometers in area) might have 30 to 100 kilometers of major streets—implying (by the simple metric above) a need for as many as several thousand soldiers simply to maintain patrols. One arrives at similar figures by looking at the size of police forces in various countries or by examining what has been done by various armies of occupation over the years. They have employed anywhere from one to ten, and in some cases as many as twenty, individuals per 1,000 local inhabitants for such purposes. The soldiers and military police would conduct activities such as patrols, cordon and search, and the establishment of checkpoints and roadblocks. They might be assisted by relatively reliable indigenous units, especially in the later stages of the operation.[17]

## The Mechanics of Seizing a Country

How would all those forces distribute themselves from their initial points of arrival in the country at issue to the various strongholds? Although the recent movement of the 1st U.S. Armored Division through Central Europe by rail may suggest that means, the general approach in hostile territory would probably be by road or air.

In-country airlift might be most appealing in a relatively large country without many major airports. In that case, the

17. Department of Public Information, United Nations, *United Nations Peace-Keeping Information Notes* (December 1994); Commandant, U.S. Army Infantry School, "The Application of Peace Enforcement Operations at Brigade and Battalion," Fort Benning, Georgia, August, 1994, p. 11; James T. Quinlivan, "Force Requirements in Stability Operations," *Parameters*, vol. 25, no. 4 (Winter 1995–1996), pp. 59–69.

intervening forces might use short-runway-capable aircraft such as C-130s as well as helicopters to get to interior sites. For such operations, the tactics of establishing smaller lodgments would be similar to those used to secure the main airfield, unless potential resistance was known to be minimal at some of the points of destination.

In the case where roads were the primary means of establishing a countrywide presence, the intervention force would need to carry out large-scale convoy transport operations. Those can be slowed or complicated by sniping, antitank fire, direct artillery fire, and mining. But they are generally only preventable when a resistance force can block or destroy bridges or other choke points, or when roads are so narrow that incapacitation of a lead convoy vehicle and a trailing vehicle can trap others. If the convoy escort was following proper doctrine—namely, using an armored heavy advance guard that deployed several kilometers in front of the main force by road or by helicopter, as well as attack helicopter reconnaissance and escort—it should usually be able to preempt or outflank any ambush, though perhaps not before suffering some losses.[18] The Soviet experience in Afghanistan and the Israeli experience in Mideast wars confirm these points.[19]

A caveat to this generally reassuring assessment of the feasibility of convoy escort operations: sophisticated resistance can make the going very difficult. Although unlikely to prevent

18. Joshua M. Epstein, *Strategy and Force Planning: The Case of the Persian Gulf* (Brookings, 1987), pp. 47–61; Commandant, U.S. Army Infantry School, "The Application of Peace Enforcement Operations at Brigade and Battalion," Fort Benning, Georgia, August, 1994, p. 24.

19. Joseph J. Collins, *The Soviet Invasion of Afghanistan* (Lexington, Mass.: Lexington Books, 1986), pp. 148-152; Scott R. McMichael, *Stumbling Bear: Soviet Military Performance in Afghanistan* (New York: Brassey's, 1991), pp. 55-57; Col Trevor N. Dupuy, ed., *International Military and Defense Encyclopedia*, vol. I (Washington, D.C.: Brassey's, 1993), p. 169. All of the aforementioned tactics were employed by the Israeli Army in capturing the Golan Heights from Syria in 1967.

the ultimate transit of convoys, it can exact a significant price in casualties. For example, Israeli forces occupying the security zone in southern Lebanon initially conducted convoy operations by road, but they took to using helicopters when Lebanese guerrillas started using remote-detonated bombs and other sophisticated tactics to attack road vehicles. And as was tragically underscored in February of 1997, when seventy-four Israeli soldiers died due to a mid-air helicopter collision, air convoys can be dangerous as well.[20] The moral of the story would seem to be that intervening troops should be very well-disciplined and proficient, in order to reduce the likelihood of successful ambush and of accident, and also that they should establish nationwide control quickly enough to prevent indigenous forces from being able to devise and implement tactics such as the above. Even then, however, casualties should be expected.

Unlike the basic Soviet approach in Afghanistan, a modern western military might also deliberately travel at night rather than in the day, since it would gain targeting advantages at that time through its night-vision and infrared sensors. If the intervention force found daytime movement necessary, it could use techniques such as smoke and concussion grenades to obscure the view and cause disorientation of any ambushing forces.

If near cities or towns, the convoy escorts would need to use special care. In attacking any enemy forces, they might first try to use precision munitions and shorter-range artillery to avoid unintended damage that, in addition to its disadvantages on humanitarian grounds, could have the tendency of setting neutral parties against the intervening force.[21]

20. See Douglas Jehl, "With Iran's Aid, Guerrillas Gain Against Israelis," *New York Times*, February 26, 1997, p. A4.

21. Headquarters, Department of the Army, *FM 100-23: Peace Operations* (December 1994), pp. 36–42; United States Army, *Ranger Handbook* (July 1992), pp. 6-13 through 6-18.

## NEUTRALIZING HOSTILE FORCES AND EXTENDING CONTROL

The final element of the operation, though not necessarily the last chronologically, would be to contain or destroy any armed groups that remained hostile even as interveners arrived. This would also be the stage of greatest relevance to cease-fires that break down after peacekeepers have deployed with the consent of indigenous parties. In some such cases, outside countries may elect to have their peacekeepers impose a peace they had previously been responsible simply for verifying. The massive killings that occurred this decade in Angola and Rwanda after peace accords collapsed show why such muscular peacekeeping may sometimes be the best way to limit casualties and hold a country together.

Depending on the nature of the conflict, lines of battle might not be sharply drawn. In some cases, containing at least certain elements of each major faction within its respective territories while keeping their enemies out could contribute to ending widespread warfare. In other cases, however, this concept of separating forces may not readily apply, and direct operations may be needed against forces that may be moving, based in close proximity to other warring parties, or otherwise difficult to quarantine.[22]

The use of force against indigenous factions should not be initiated lightly. As John Hirsch and Robert Oakley, drawing on their experience with recent operations in Somalia and elsewhere, write:

> A peacekeeping or peace enforcement operation may involve a strong military presence, with authority to use force if necessary, but it has of necessity been a maxim of peacekeeping that every effort must be made not to make enemies, or to be seen as taking

22. Headquarters, Department of the Army, *FM 100-23: Peace Operations* (December 1994), p. 11; *Field Manual 100-20 and Air Force Pamphlet 3-20: Military Operations in Low Intensity Conflict*, pp. 2-24 through 2-25.

sides in an internal confrontation. Even if some immediate military reaction should be necessary—for example, in response to an attack on peacekeepers—it should not lead to long-term hostility with any group.[23]

There is clearly much to be said for the logic of this position. And it would almost always be the best thing an intervening force could do for its *own* security—short of staying home and not intervening in the first place.

Taken to its logical extreme, however, such an attitude would seem to confer what might be termed strategic immunity on an extremist and violent group. Such a group could harass and test the outside forces. At worst, it would receive only modest tactical reprisals as a consequence, probably then concluding that it should wait until the interveners left before resuming full-fledged pursuit of power. At best, it might establish the upper hand and cause severe political problems for the coalition of outside forces, perhaps leading to its premature withdrawal or otherwise severely limiting its effectiveness. Thus, for the cases considered here that fall fully within the UN's Chapter VII guidelines of forceful intervention, a studiously neutral pose may sometimes be unwise. And battlefield escalation may sometimes make sense.

Two main strategies could be attempted in order to defeat an extremist indigenous group. One is to assume that a unified indigenous military or police, formed or strengthened during the occupation stage of the operation, would be able to fend them off after the outside forces departed. The other is for interveners actively to pursue those destabilizing forces as part and parcel of their intervention.

Determining which strategy to pursue, and when, is one of the most important matters for the interveners to wrestle with. Any decision would presumably be informed partly by what

23. John L. Hirsch and Robert B. Oakley, *Somalia and Operation Restore Hope* (Washington, D.C.: U.S. Institute of Peace, 1995), p. 157.

was known about indigenous groups before the intervention; partly by how they behaved in the very initial stages of the deployment; and partly by how they acted as it unfolded. A group with an extremely ruthless leader such as Idi Amin should generally be opposed from the start, as might groups such as the Khmer Rouge or Rwandan Hutu extremists. A clan led by the likes of a General Aideed, or Charles Taylor in Liberia, might not be so obviously worse than the alternatives as to engender immediate opposition. But if the group attacked outside forces, or blatantly pursued its own power at the expense of efforts at political reconciliation, it might later be singled out for attack.

This issue highlights the difficulty of using military tools to stop deadly conflict. If an extremist and violent group is constantly maneuvering for position and is uninterested in anything short of its own ultimate hold on power, it would be highly risky to leave that group strong and cohesive. But if the operation is pursued too soon, with unclear rationale, it may take on the trappings of a vendetta that could stiffen the resolve of the attacked group and even improve its ability to engender domestic sympathy and recruit new members. A quickness to the trigger on the part of interveners might also lead various groups to try to deceive the outside force into attacking their rivals.[24]

What types of indigenous military capabilities are the outside forces likely to face? Even the larger non-Western militaries are generally poor on air power, logistics sustainability,

24. For a classic argument along these "hearts and minds" lines, see Sir Robert Thompson, *Defeating Communist Insurgency* (New York: Praeger, 1966), pp. 50–58; also see Headquarters of the Departments of the Army and Air Force, *Field Manual 100-20 and Air Force Pamphlet 3-20: Military Operations in Low Intensity Conflict* (December 1990), pp. 2-9, 2-24; and Herbert Howe, "Lessons of Liberia: ECOMOG and Regional Peacekeeping," *International Security*, vol. 21, no. 3 (Winter 1996/97), pp. 145–76.

combined-arms operations, and strategic planning.[25] These conclusions are even more germane for the types of bands, clans, and militias that are likely to be at issue when forcible humanitarian intervention is considered. The marksmanship, bravery, dedication, unit cohesiveness, and tactics of hostile forces will vary in quality from situation to situation. But certain capabilities will simply not be found in these types of settings.

Although the outside militaries would likely suffer casualties in ambushes and other attacks, their combined-arms capabilities and enveloping operations would give them a substantial advantage under most circumstances. Indirect fire from artillery and fuel-air explosives and the like could prevent indigenous factions, once located and targeted, from safely maneuvering or otherwise remaining exposed. Helicopters and AC-130 gunships, together with fighting vehicles and infantry weapons, would allow for accurate three-dimensional direct fire. Use of counterartillery radars, night-vision equipment, infrared detection devices, and possibly even Joint STARS aircraft would make targeting easier and fire even more accurate. Helicopters would also provide aerial monitoring of the battlefield and the capability for rapid insertion of troops into or out of combat positions.[26]

The types of specific small-unit tactics that outside forces would use to attack or to respond to ambush when themselves surprised are fairly straightforward. Scouting teams would

25. See, for example, Anthony H. Cordesman and Abraham R. Wagner, *The Lessons of Modern War*, vol. II (Boulder, Colo.: 1990), pp. 40–63.

26. Improvements in self-protection capabilities are also being made in the wake of the U.S. military operations of the past fifteen years and in particular after Somalia. HUMVEE utility vehicles are being given armor to protect against mines; Bradley fighting vehicles are being given new armored tiles to protect against rocket-propelled grenades; tanks are being used when necessary. General Accounting Office, *Peace Operations: Effect of Training, Equipment, and Other Factors on Unit Capability*, GAO/NSIAD-96-14 (October 1995), pp. 40–41.

attempt to locate enemy forces. Once the enemy was found, a base of fire including machine guns and artillery would be established by one unit. Others would then conduct flanking maneuvers, often under screening by smoke grenades. Those maneuvers would be executed quickly. Various elements of the company, platoon, or squad conducting the attack would stagger their activities—including movements, firings, and reloadings—to ensure a sustained pace of attack and to cover for each other. As noted, technological advantages such as helicopters, night-vision goggles, and counterartillery radars would be of great help in the mission. But it would be as much fundamental infantry fighting skills—high tempo of operations, marksmanship, effective use of artillery, coordinated maneuver on foot, reliable and rapid communication between platoons or squads, properly overlapping fields of fire, proper use of camouflage and smoke and concussion grenades to obscure flanking movements, and the like—that would make or break the battles.[27]

A very good indigenous force, even without air support or the most modern weaponry, could make operations very difficult for a better-equipped force by fighting from defensive postures. Doing so is made possible by proper tactics, unit cohesion, staying power, and marksmanship, as demonstrated by experiences during the highly realistic exercises at the Army's Joint Readiness Training Center at Fort Polk and other facilities.[28] By fighting in smaller units, generally avoiding pitched battle, and using terrain or urban settings as well as civilian populations for cover or camouflage, groups armed only lightly can extract substantial casualties. (For example, even with

27. United States Army, *Ranger Handbook* (Fort Benning, Ga.: U.S. Army Infantry School, 1992), pp. 6-2 through 6-40; Congressional Budget Office, *An Analysis of U.S. Army Helicopter Programs* (December 1995), pp. 5–7; John F. Schmitt, *Mastering Tactics* (Quantico, Va.: Marine Corps Association, 1994), pp. 42–55.

28. See Brig. Gen. Robert H. Scales Jr., *Certain Victory: The U.S. Army in the Gulf War* (Washington, D.C.: Brassey's, 1994), pp. 20–23.

U.S. reconnaissance planes frequently in the air over Mogadishu in 1993, only about two mortars were quickly spotted and destroyed over a period during which about sixty shots were fired by Somali irregulars.)[29]

Resistance forces may also completely eschew traditional combat and focus on terrorism. This will generally not impede outside forces in establishing general order, though it can certainly increase their casualties and sustain a certain level of fear and mistrust within a society. Indigenous security forces may eventually be capable of keeping a lid on such insurgent activities themselves—though if they have to contend with resistance from a major political and military group, the prospects for longer-term stability may be mediocre. For example, dedicated terrorist units of even tens or hundreds of people can perpetrate a great deal of violence in urban settings and other frequented areas.[30] Witness, for example, the success of Hamas and other Mideast terrorist organizations despite the best efforts of Israeli intelligence.[31]

By using such tactics, indigenous forces may be able to bleed outside forces to the point where the mission no longer seems worth the cost to them and is prematurely curtailed. This is clearly a strategy that has recently vindicated itself against major military establishments in places such as Lebanon, Afghanistan, and Somalia. Again, the analysis returns to a point made at the outset: the paramount importance of avoiding

29. "U.S. Military Operations in Somalia," Hearings before the U.S. Senate Committee on Armed Services, S. Hrg. 103-846, May 12, 1994, p. 41.

30. James J. Gallagher, *Low-Intensity Conflict: A Guide for Tactics, Techniques, and Procedures* (Harrisburg, Pa.: Stackpole Books, 1992), pp. 71–73.

31. Islamic fundamentalist terrorists in the Middle East number in the hundreds, or perhaps at most the low thousands, in all. They are generally organized into "cells," of which there are probably several score in the region, each including anywhere from a handful to several dozen individuals. See Youssef M. Ibrahim, "The Twin Towers: Terrorism; throughout Arab World, 20 Years of Growth," *New York Times*, March 6, 1993, p. B24.

turning the war into a guerrilla-style engagement. That challenge is more political art than military science, reinforcing this study's theme that techniques of military analysis, though illuminating, cannot by themselves resolve the principal question of whether a given operation is likely to succeed at modest cost.

## SUMMING UP THE REQUIREMENTS

In the above discussion, approximate numbers of troops required for specific missions have often been discussed. In addition, it has often been stated or assumed that those intervening forces should be of a certain high quality to establish the types of superiority likely to be needed to prevail decisively in infantry combat engagements. What do these considerations imply more specifically about the numbers of forces needed for an intervention and the training, equipping, and related preparation they should have received?

### Size of Force

In aggregate, an intervening force's size is determined by three principal issues: the demands of expected combat engagements; the demands of policing and other routine "presence" activities that create a climate of security; and the need to supply the forces carrying out the first two activities. The first generally requires combat forces, though they may be regular units or special forces, depending on the nature of the mission, together with their direct combat support, such as engineers. The second requires combat forces, special forces, or military police; the last demands support units as well as additional combat units to protect their operations.

The starting point for force sizing is the general rule that outside forces should usually be comparable in total numbers to the largest potential opposition they could face in battle. It may seem surprising that one would not call for outright quantitative superiority. But, given the outside force's presumed advantages in mobility, it would often be able to fight with numerical superiority nonetheless—not to mention its advantages in firepower and other areas. In addition, in infantry combat militaries generally strive to use units of comparable size to those they are opposing in order to retain tactical flexibility and avoid muddling the battlefield.[32]

In Somalia in 1993, for example, U.S. forces numbering only about 2,000 combat troops (of which 440 were Rangers) pursued General Aideed's many thousands of partisans subsequent to the June 5, 1993, massacre of twenty-four Pakistani peacekeepers.[33] Yet senior military commanders did not attribute the difficulties encountered by U.S. forces to their modest numbers. They felt that the United States was in military terms winning the war when it chose for broader policy reasons to end its manhunt for Aideed and to disengage from the country.[34] Much is made of the fact that U.S. forces might well have benefited from more use of armored vehicles and from greater numbers of AC-130 gunships. But even in the ill-fated firefight in Mogadishu in October of 1993, they had clear military superiority.

More than raw size, it is the ability of forces to deploy quickly, to seal off potential enemy avenues of reinforcement, to locate and target opposition, and to attack in a coordinated and concentrated manner that determines the success of an operation of this sort.[35]

32. Gallagher, Low-Intensity Conflict, p. 43.

33. See Terrence Lyons and Ahmed I. Samatar, Somalia: State Collapse, Multilateral Intervention, and Strategies for Political Reconstruction (Brookings, 1995), pp. 1–24, 77–79.

34. "U.S. Military Operations in Somalia," Hearings before the U.S. Senate Committee on Armed Services, S. Hrg. 103-846, May 12, 1994, pp. 17, 38–39, 62–63.

35. See Gallagher, Low-Intensity Conflict, p. 54.

Requisite numbers of forces also are a function of the size and topography of the country at issue. These factors determine the policing and monitoring capabilities that interveners must possess in addition to their tactical combat superiority.

How great are the needs here? It varies with the situation, but some general rules of thumb and analogies are helpful. Take, for example, policing capabilities in some Western countries today, or the size of occupation forces that were needed to police Germany after the general surrender of its armed forces in 1945. In these cases, one arrives at a rule of roughly two to three police per 1,000 inhabitants. In other more tense places, such as counterinsurgency efforts today in the Punjab of India or the 1965 U.S. occupation of the Dominican Republic, five or six police or soldiers per 1,000 inhabitants were deemed necessary. In more extreme cases, British counterinsurgency efforts in colonial Malaya and Northern Ireland employed about twenty personnel per 1,000 inhabitants. For a country of 10 million, these experiences imply a need for at least 20,000 troops, unless indigenous help is immediately available for policing purposes.

These numbers are not dissimilar from those needed in the United States today in peacetime. In the United States, there are roughly 1 million law enforcement officers for a population of 260 million, or four per 1,000. Somewhat smaller ratios of forces are found in places such as Haiti, where a 7,000 person force has served a population of 7 million, and in a number of other developing countries. In general, providing internal security requires one to five law enforcement officers per 1,000 inhabitants.[36]

A corollary of these observations, emphasized elsewhere by James T. Quinlivan, is that intervention of the type discussed

36. See for example, U.S. Department of Justice, *Law Enforcement Management and Administrative Statistics, 1993: Data for Individual State and Local Agencies with 100 or More Officers* (1993), pp. 1–12.

in this study is generally impracticable in large countries. It will generally be practicable only if an indigenous security force can be cobbled together early in an operation to provide for basic safety and law and order, while outside forces provide only the firepower needed to deal with any concerted opposition.[37]

Proper numbers of troops can also depend on the nonmilitary and nonsecurity tasks that might be needed in a country suffering from starvation or some other violence-related humanitarian crisis. But the assumption here is that most of those would be passed off to civilian relief agencies as soon as possible and would not constitute a major concern for military planners. The military force would in that case simply provide protection to certain civilian activities, notably for convoys, relief distribution, and the like.

Also, a force needs to be sized largely in terms of the support capabilities that appear at various levels of aggregation of the military force—from battalion to brigade to division. Generally speaking, an intervening force needs to include most of the assets associated with a divisional structure, such as its engineering, aviation, communications, and transport companies and other specialized units. Capabilities such as loading and unloading equipment for ports and airfields may also be required.

Indeed, it is support capabilities that generally place the greatest numerical demands on intervening forces. Usually, combat forces of a given number require more than twice as many individuals for support. The arithmetic relations behind this ratio of "tooth to tail" can be seen in the force structure of the U.S. Army. Ten active Army divisions possess among them roughly 170,000 troops in a service about 500,000 strong. One should subtract a number of active-duty individuals performing

37. Quinlivan, "Force Requirements in Stability Operations," pp. 59–69.

central activities such as weapons acquisition and some types of intelligence gathering and analysis. However, the active forces rely on reserves for some additional support as well.[38] And the typical deployment could require even more support units than the average mission, given the austere conditions to be expected in many countries where forcible humanitarian interventions might be undertaken.

## Quality of Forces

As noted, the above force sizings presume a substantial qualitative advantage for intervening forces over indigenous units. How does one determine whether or not a given unit meets the appropriate standards—not only for combat capabilities but for the ability to sustain itself in a foreign land and to behave with the levels of professionalism and restraint required for an operation that in broader terms is at least as much political as military?

Short of war itself, the U.S. military has a number of realistic combat training exercises that can be used to evaluate units. Conceivably, other countries' forces could be tested at the National Military Training Centers; they already are to some degree present there, and they fly a number of exercises at the tactical aircraft training schools. But such collaboration at U.S. facilities will be constrained by their limited availability and in any case provide only a final confirmation of ability rather than a regimen for step-by-step improvement.

The Joint Chiefs of Staff use three criteria to evaluate U.S. forces: readiness, sustainability, and modernization. The latter is

38. Congressional Budget Office, *An Analysis of U.S. Army Helicopter Programs* (December 1995), p. 66; *Organization of the United States Army*, p. M-1; Department of Defense, *Defense Almanac 94* (Washington, D.C.: Government Printing Office, 1994), pp. 24–25; Congressional Budget Office, "An Analysis of the Army's Force Structure: Summary" (April 1997), p. 6.

the simplest and pertains to basic caliber of combat equipment. Sustainability, probably the Achilles' heel of most militaries in the world today, involves equipment such as trucks, port and airfield loading and unloading equipment, medical facilities, water purification systems, and the like, as well as combat sustainability in realms of ammunition, spare parts, and fuel. At present, very few western militaries are capable of supporting themselves at great distances from their own territories.[39] The participation of the United States, or at least France or Britain, is for that reason generally a prerequisite to establishing and continuing any major operation of division size or greater overseas (unless most support is available from the local economy—as it generally is in peacekeeping operations, but generally would not be for the forcible interventions at issue here).

Readiness refers to the immediate operating status of equipment, and to the attributes and training experience of troops themselves. Those troops need to have followed months of intensive training according to a modern and rigorous military doctrine and to have had several weeks' preparation for the specific type of operation at hand.

In addition to these unit-level demands, any successful operation also needs effective command and control at three distinct levels. The first is the strategic level, where military experts and top officials translate political mandates into broad military objectives. The next two are the operational level, akin to the U.S. regional command system, where a broad sense of day-to-day operations is maintained; and the tactical level, where general direction is translated into specific duties for individual units.[40]

39. Stephen T. Sargeant, "Force Shaping: The Key to Cost Effective Cooperative Security," *National Security Studies Quarterly*, vol. 2, no. 1 (Winter 1996), pp. 37–57.

40. See David S. Alberts and Richard E. Hayes, *Command Arrangements for Peace Operations* (Washington, D.C.: National Defense University, 1995), pp. 50, 70.

Finding well-trained forces led by officers familiar with proper counterinsurgency tactics and procedures is not easy. By both measures, the Soviet military in Afghanistan fell short, and by the latter measure the U.S. intervention in Vietnam as well as the French attempt to hold on to Algeria failed. Again, one is left with the conclusion that at least one top-notch western military, preferably that of the United States, is needed to make a forcible intervention work.[41]

At the same time, one may also need to accommodate the political pressures to include a wide array of foreign forces. Doing so can give an operation greater legitimacy and international support. Marine Corps General Anthony Zinni, experienced in both Operation Provide Comfort in Iraq and Operation Restore Hope in Somalia, had to help forge viable coalitions out of the militaries of thirteen and twenty-four nations, respectively, in those two instances. Despite the difficulties of doing so, he saw advantages:

> In Somalia the first time around, we had the forces of eight nations defending the airfield. Was that because that airfield was so big or so threatened? No. It was because the forces of those eight nations could go no farther than that airfield when they got off the airplane. For either political or military reasons, that was about it. But they got participation points; and obviously the sense of international legitimacy that is given to you is important.[42]

Whether redundant guarding of a central airfield is generally a useful employment of suboptimal troops is open to some doubt. But there are also other purposes to which good but less

---

41. For a well-documented and penetrating critique of U.S. military policy in the Vietnam War—and expressions of concern that some trends in recent Army thinking for lower-intensity operations remain misguided—see Andrew F. Krepinevich Jr., *The Army and Vietnam* (Johns Hopkins University Press, 1986), pp. 258–75.

42. Lieutenant General Anthony Zinni, U.S. Marine Corps, "It's Not Nice and Neat," *Proceedings*, August 1995, p. 30.

than top-notch forces could certainly be put. Notably, the patrolling and military police functions—often the chief factors pushing up the requisite size of an overall force—can be performed by well-disciplined and individually competent soldiers even if their abilities to conduct tactical combined-arms combat operations are limited. These types of operations may be within the capabilities of the better forces from certain countries in South Asia, smaller countries in Europe, and at least a few Latin American and African militaries. The best of those forces might also be able to assist with somewhat more difficult operations such as site security for communications, energy, transportation, and water infrastructure.

It is probably only in the realms of tactically offensive operations, as well as activities such as punching a convoy through an ambush, where the best forces are required. But in those situations, top-quality forces are essential to the mission's success, at least as the spearhead and principal rapid-reaction force of any operation. Poor forces could lose aircraft at the initial point of arrival, fail to overcome ambushes of convoys, fail to reach interior points of the country in a timely fashion, and frequently lose firefights with indigenous forces, possibly emboldening the latter to initiate more.

When all is said and done, top-caliber units will generally have to represent a large fraction of the total intervening force, perhaps half or more. To the extent requirements for top-caliber combat forces as well as major logistics and transport units can be separated from those for site security and policing, the calculation can be made directly and the best forces used primarily for the first set of missions. More often, the respective demands from these two different categories of operations will not be so easily weighed. Planners will in that case have to make conservative assumptions about the possible demands on combat forces and logistics units and build in a margin of insurance.

If interveners enjoyed larger numerical advantages than discussed above, their quantitative advantage could to some extent compensate for their limited qualitative capabilities. But precise and effective assaults against radical forces could still be needed. Artillery barrages against whole sections of a city, indiscriminate killings of suspected guerrillas, or other techniques historically used by an occupier against a determined indigenous foe are generally ineffective. They would also be at variance with the basic humanitarian purpose of an intervention to restore order or to overthrow a brutal regime. There is no substitute, in the end, for highly competent combat troops and intelligence personnel in these types of operations.

# 3
# MANDATES, EXIT STRATEGIES, AND MISSION DURATION

U sing military force to restore security is inherently far more than a military operation. There is no implied or de facto mission that an outside force is naturally supporting by becoming involved. Even in cases where a cease-fire or peace accord had existed but then been violated, and peacekeepers sought to enforce respect for the cease-fire, new decisions would be needed. To wit, should those parties that violated the accord be invited back into the peace process or thereafter considered as adversaries of both the intervening force and a new indigenous government? Any military mission of this type can make sense only in the context of a broader political strategy.[1]

This set of issues is largely separable from the mechanics of a deployment as outlined in chapter 2. But it is inextricably linked in policy terms to the technical operations considered there. What is more, the subject of chapter 4—the costs and

1. For a similar view, see David Ramsbotham, "The Changing Nature of Intervention," Conflict Studies 282, Research Institute for the Study of Conflict and Terrorism, London, England, p. 21.

casualties of any intervention—can only be broached once some means of thinking about the likely duration of a deployment is established, as well as the scope of military operations to be conducted once a general sense of order and security has been restored. That raises the issue of exit strategies.

Several broad conclusions emerge from this chapter. First, the mechanics of what is sometimes derisively called "nation-building"—revamping a country's security forces, for example, as well as its courts and other basic institutions—are admittedly difficult. But they can at least be set to a rough schedule. Typically, military interventions followed by efforts to reform a country's key institutions can be expected to last one and a half to two years after basic security is established. In many cases outside troops will not have to carry out these efforts, but they will need to provide security for them.

However, following a schedule may prove infeasible if one or more strong renegade factions remain outside any political reconciliation effort in a country. In fact, it is quite unlikely to be achievable in cases like Bosnia, where large competing armies are tolerated under the mandate of a peacekeeping or intervention force. And it appears to have failed recently in Cambodia, where the decision to allow Hun Sen's forces continued legitimacy rather than force their demobilization helped make possible Sen's July 1997 coup.

In some such cases, partition of the territory at issue may provide a solution. There are pros and cons to such an approach. On the one hand, a partition that one side does not accept, or that divides territory in a way that leaves some significant lands contested, may not prove stabilizing—as continued disputes over lands like Kashmir, Northern Ireland, and the Golan Heights demonstrate (to say nothing of the divisions of China and Korea). On the other hand, without either partition or a schedule to demobilize opposing armies and form a new integrated structure and government, negotiations and peacekeeping missions will usually establish more of a cease-fire than a peace.

Finally, decisions on whether outside forces should pursue war criminals or keep certain types of parties and individuals out of elections are hard to reach in the abstract. In many situations civil wars have ended without punishment for major abusers of human rights or military leaders. As long as they are pushed from office, limited to symbolic roles or power sharing, or at least forced to compete in free and monitored elections, they may not be impediments to peace. Examples are the continued presence of Pinochet in Chile, de Klerk in South Africa, and Ortega in Nicaragua.

But in other cases, leaving old powers in place will not work. Either a ruler or a regime will be too brutal to be trustworthy in the eyes of its fellow citizens and the international community (Idi Amin, Pol Pot, and the interahamwe in Rwanda) or they may be too bent on absolute rule to be plausible candidates for participation in a democratic process (Aideed in Somalia and the junta in Haiti). In those cases, particularly the former types of situations, if outside forces have good enough intelligence to make successful attacks against such individuals and their core supporters, there is a strong argument to accept the risks associated with carrying them out.

## When Not to Intervene

Before exploring the specific ways in which an intervention's prospects can be made as good as possible, it is the better part of wisdom to underline when they should not be attempted. Much of what is said here is implicit in other parts of this study but worth special emphasis. In some cases, the wisest mission mandate is no mandate, and the best exit strategy is not to enter in the first place.

Forcible interventions should not be considered unless a certain threshold of violence has been reached or seems likely to be reached. Most civil wars in the world today have casualty rates roughly comparable to the U.S. murder rate, meaning that their bloodshed—however regrettable—is not severe enough to justify the application of such a crude and dangerous instrument of policy as a major multilateral military deployment.[2]

Second, intervention for humanitarian purposes should not be attempted in countries or regions where it could make a wider war involving major powers more likely. That would defeat the basic humanitarian rationale of the missions considered here. To take a couple of historical examples, fighting to liberate Tibet or to end the carnage in Chechnya would not have been wise.

Third, intervention should usually not be attempted in situations where it is simply too unlikely that a country's politics can be stabilized and where factions are committed and very violent. Leaving behind a well-functioning democracy in a country is often an unrealistic goal, to be sure. But leaving behind a security landscape in which war is likely to resume once interveners depart can only be sensible policy in extreme cases. One such exceptional case was Somalia in 1992, where famine made the death rate from the "complex humanitarian emergency" far greater than from the shooting, and ending the temporary food shortage was a worthy goal in itself. If war can be expected to resume once outside troops leave, however, a humanitarian intervention probably does not make sense in most cases.

2. See Stockholm International Peace Research Institute, *SIPRI Yearbook 1996* (New York: Oxford University Press, 1996), pp. 24–30; International Negotiation Network, *State of World Conflict Report 1994–1995* (Atlanta, Ga.: Carter Center, 1995); Stephen J. Solarz and Michael E. O'Hanlon, "Humanitarian Intervention: When Force Is Justified," *Washington Quarterly*, vol. 20, no. 4 (Autumn 1997).

For example, intervention seems unwise in Afghanistan, even if the war there continues for some time. That sad country deserves better than its lot of the past two decades, but the challenges to forcible intervention are just too great. Not only would getting there require either extremely difficult transit across mountains—assuming that a neighboring country would even be willing to allow a staging base on its territory— or massive and continual airlift operations, but it is also very hard to think of how a number of extremist groups, most supported by Iran, fundamentalist in character, or both, could be induced to cooperate with outside powers. Operating within the country would also be difficult and dangerous, given the battle toughness of various factions, their expertise in convoy ambush operations, and their possession of Stinger anti-aircraft missiles.

Fourth, humanitarian interventions should not seek to defeat very strong armies supported by mass movements. In other words, they should avoid revolutions (as in Iran in the late 1970s), guerrilla struggles (as in Vietnam in the 1960s), and highly ideological conflicts where outsiders might become associated with a disliked indigenous group (as in Lebanon in the early 1980s).[3]

Fifth, interventions should usually not be undertaken in highly populous countries unless an indigenous security force can be quickly salvaged and enlisted in policing work. Being in control of a country requires more than being the strongest military force on its territory; it also requires ensuring that no major security vacuums develop. Accomplishing this goal takes at a bare minimum 1 police officer per 1,000 population—or 100,000 individuals (and perhaps even two or three times that

---

3. Richard N. Haass, *Intervention: The Use of American Military Force in the Post–Cold War World* (Washington, D.C.: Carnegie Endowment, 1994), pp. 23–24, 83–84, 104–05; Neil Sheehan, *A Bright Shining Lie* (New York: Random House, 1988), pp. 127–265.

number) in a country of 100 million.[4] Consequently, interventions in countries such as Nigeria, Bangladesh, Pakistan, Brazil, and Indonesia would be next to impossible without indigenous help; interventions in India and China would be just about unthinkable.

## TO NATION-BUILD, NATION-DIVIDE, NEGOTIATE, OR NEUTRALIZE?

The above considerations exclude from the scope of this analysis the vast majority of civil wars, nevertheless leaving a considerable number as candidates for forcible humanitarian intervention.

What mission mandates and exit strategies would make sense in cases where the United States and other outside countries did decide to quell violence and reestablish stability in a country? Given the robust interventions considered in this study, one would expect that policymakers would think ambitiously about their political goals.

For example, the reconstruction or at least the fundamental improvement of a country's national security institutions would generally be appropriate, since it would often have been their incompetence or inhumaneness that helped provoke the intervention in the first place. But other questions would remain. Should war criminals be arrested? Should certain factional armies be deliberately weakened through battlefield attack even at the risk of substantial casualties to intervening forces? Should certain types of political parties or associations be banned? Should a representative mix of individuals of various ethnic or regional associations be insisted on for any subse-

4. James T. Quinlivan, "Force Requirements in Stability Operations," *Parameters*, vol. 25, no. 4 (Winter 1995–96), pp. 59–69.

quent indigenous government? Should the country even be partitioned?

This is not the place to conduct an exhaustive assessment of all these issues. But the degree to which they affect military decisionmaking and military risk is important for the present purposes, and basic tradeoffs need to be highlighted.

Resolving tradeoffs is very difficult in practice. Consider the degree to which even the militarily and politically astute Colin Powell was torn over proper U.S. policy in Somalia. Often associated with the doctrines of using overwhelming force and intervening only to defend clear American interests, Powell's actual views are more complex, particularly as concerns Somalia in 1992–93.[5] That intervention occurred nearly entirely while Powell was chairman of the Joint Chiefs of Staff, and it is fair to assume that he weighed in on every major policy decision except those *after* the fateful firefight of October 3, 1993, in which eighteen Americans lost their lives (his tenure as chairman of the Joint Chiefs of Staff ended in late September 1993).

Powell's views on the subject include his initial idea that a rapid withdrawal from Somalia would probably have invited a rekindling of anarchy and violence, and later that American military commanders involved in the pursuit of General Aideed warranted more firepower and armor to get the job done. But he also felt a gnawing sense that the nation-building/manhunt missions did not make good sense and merited fresh scrutiny.[6]

---

5. For evidence, see Colin L. Powell, "U.S. Forces: Challenges Ahead," *Foreign Affairs*, vol. 72, no. 5 (Winter 1992/1993); for the more absolutist version of the doctrine of highly selective and overwhelming use of force, see Caspar W. Weinberger, "The Uses of Military Power," Remarks to the National Press Club, November 28, 1984.

6. See Colin L. Powell, *My American Journey* (New York: Random House, 1995), pp. 564–65, 580–84.

## War Criminals

Just as Powell recognized the difficulty of determining sound policy vis-à-vis Somalia and General Aideed, it is hard to know if vigorous pursuit of war criminals in Bosnia or Rwanda would affect those countries' prospects for peace. Weakening or capturing the principal antagonists would presumably help—though it could also embitter or render paranoid the remaining partisans of the war criminals, thereby hardening their determination to fight on rather than run the risks of attempting political reconciliation.

What is more, arresting war criminals might have only limited beneficial effect if they were replaced by equally extreme or aggressive leaders or if other potential causes of renewed war remained unresolved. For example, as long as the contradiction remains between claiming that Bosnia is a unified state and allowing two or three separate armies to coexist within it, it is hard to know if the absence from the scene of Radovan Karadzic or Ratko Mladic would appreciably reduce the odds of remaining Serbs' (or other groups') fighting for the Brcko corridor or some other stake.[7] Civil wars in places like Central America and southern Africa have generally ended even though those who fought them, and often committed atrocities in the process, remained free. Similarly, peace and more humane politics appear entrenched in southern South America despite not bringing to justice those who perpetrated violence against their own citizens in the past. By contrast, war in Somalia continues even after General Aideed Sr.'s death; tensions remain acute in Korea even after the passing of Kim Il-Sung; and the overthrow of Idi Amin hardly brought peace to Uganda.

---

7. For a very cogent discussion of peace operations in Bosnia, see Stephen John Stedman, "'The Exit Is the Strategy': IFOR in Bosnia," unpublished paper, 1996.

Still, it often makes sense to drive tyrants out of power if for no other reason than to give countries a fresh start (and to help justify the intervention in the eyes of foreign publics). Forcing out Haiti's junta in 1994 clearly improved political conditions in that country—largely because democratically legitimated, if flawed, individuals were on hand to pick up the reins of power. Success was less striking in Panama in some ways, though even there some political stability has emerged and the growth of GDP has improved substantially since the overthrow of Mañuel Noriega.[8]

## Partition

Another important issue is whether or not, in the process of helping restore indigenous rule and order, outsiders should consider allowing partition of a country. Some argue that, in countries with relatively clear lines of ethnic division and identities, partition can be a wise course. In cases where hatred and fear drive conflict more than imperial or territorial ambition, they argue, partition may be able to defuse the dynamics and paranoias of the security dilemma.[9] It may also facilitate a clear exit strategy and an approximate exit schedule while providing an improved chance for peace. Also, the international community has leverage to pressure the new governments to ensure respect for minority rights, to promote interstate commerce between the new countries, and to pledge not to resolve outstanding territo-

8. World Bank, *World Development Report 1996: From Plan to Market* (Oxford: Oxford University Press, 1996), p. 209.

9. For other articulations of this type of viewpoint, see Chaim Kaufmann, "Possible and Impossible Solutions to Ethnic Civil Wars," *International Security*, vol. 20, no. 4 (Spring 1996), pp. 136–75; Francis M. Deng, "Blood Brothers," *Brookings Review*, vol. 13, no. 3 (Summer 1995), pp. 12–17; Thomas L. Friedman, "The Double Anschluss," *New York Times*, March 27, 1996, p. A21; John J. Mearsheimer and Stephen Van Evera, "Hateful Neighbors," *New York Times*, September 24, 1996, p. A25.

rial disputes through violence. Getting them to do so may mitigate the most severe dangers and downsides of partition.[10]

Others point out, however, that even in cases where ethnic
groups are relatively well separated, partition may not resolve
specific matters of contention (like Kashmir in India, or the
Brcko corridor in Bosnia). Partition also may not work in cases
where at least one ethnic group feels a historical right to complete control over all territory at issue (like many Arabs at the
time of the creation of Israel, the Han Chinese in Tibet, or the
Greeks and Turks in Cyprus).[11]

Whether or not partition provides a permanent solution, in
some cases it may help temporarily—possibly allowing enough
time for new leaders who may be better able to devise lasting
peace agreements to arrive on the scene. This approach can
work if the international community remains engaged with
peacekeeping forces; if those who seek to overturn partition
and reunify a territory under their own rule are weaker than
those content with partition, as in the Syrian-Israeli conflict; or
if the countries involved are led by cautious leaders, as may
now be the case with India and Pakistan concerning Kashmir.

In the abstract, this debate cannot be resolved. Powerful
examples can be mustered to support either the propartition or
the antipartition argument. But at least one general point can be
established: interventions in unified countries that retain several
competing factions of comparable strength are unlikely to be
concluded according to a set schedule.[12] In cases such as Bosnia
and Central Africa, where significant competing forces are tolerated or even legitimated by the workings of outsiders, the need
for a third party to act as an honest broker can go on indefinitely.

By contrast, it is generally the case that missions in coun-

---

10. For similar views, see Haass, *Intervention*, p. 119.

11. For such an argument, see Radha Kumar, "Partition's Troubled History,"
*Foreign Affairs*, vol. 76, no. 1 (January/February 1997), pp. 22–34.

12. I am indebted to Stephen Stedman for this point.

tries following peace implementation plans like those in Mozambique or Namibia—where a single armed force and government is accepted in principle by parties to a peace accord and then buttressed by outsiders—can be set to a schedule and keep that schedule. This is demonstrated in more detail below for the specific elements of so-called state building—holding elections, training police and army forces, rebuilding justice systems, and initiating economic recovery.

## BASIC ELEMENTS OF NATION-BUILDING AND NATION-REPAIRING

To eliminate the immediate causes of whatever conflict outside forces were sent to contain, political stability as well as reliability and professionalism in the ranks of the country's security and legal institutions would generally be prerequisites. The scope of what would be needed can give an indication of the likely duration of any operation serving those purposes.

### Elections

It may not behoove countries with a history of severe antagonism or violence along class, ethnic, or regional lines to institute simple winner-take-all majority rule. Requiring coalition governments to have quotas for different groups, as well as checks and balances in their governments and broad representation at the top levels of the military and police, might be wise policy. These goals might in turn be served by encouraging the formation of broad-based political parties and even banning those that identify themselves ethnically, religiously, or regionally.[13]

13. Other mechanisms for instituting political moderation might also be wise. For example, as a check on popular but extremist parties such as Algeria's fundamentalists, it might be wise to disallow constitutional changes for a number of years—perhaps two election cycles—after any intervention force leaves.

Peace operations have succeeded, at least in relative terms, where an Aristide was available and willing to represent national interests and rule with relative clemency and fairness; they have failed in places like Somalia and Afghanistan, where such an individual was lacking. So individuals do matter. Making it possible for civic-minded leaders to attain and hold power is a key ingredient of any mission, for without such leaders the mission is likely to fail.[14] And being willing to limit the goals of an intervention—or even to choose not to carry out the intervention—may be the better part of valor and wisdom in cases where good leaders are lacking.

If a reasonable set of candidates and parties is already available, elections can generally be organized and held in a matter of months. In other cases, where tensions and antagonisms remain high or new political parties need to be given a chance to develop, the process may take a year or more. But only rarely should it take longer than that.[15]

## Security Forces

Local security forces must also be established rapidly. More to the point, selection and training for those forces must begin early because those efforts take a fair amount of time to complete. It is critical that the force be unbiased, widely respected, and professional—difficult goals to attain anywhere, particularly in war-torn societies.

14. For a similar view from an experienced practitioner of peace operations, see Testimony of Lt. General Anthony Zinni, U.S. Marine Corps, before the House Committee on National Security, November 8, 1995.

15. See, for example, Department of Public Information, United Nations, *United Nations Peace-Keeping Information Notes* (New York: December 1994), p. 48, pp. 123–24 (on El Salvador and Mozambique); Virginia Page Fortna, "United Nations Angola Verification Mission II," in William J. Durch, ed., *The Evolution of UN Peacekeeping* (New York: St. Martin's Press, 1993), p. 393.

For these types of service, training requirements are on the order of six months to a year, once a pool of politically screened individuals has been formed. That amount of time is not enough to build top-caliber forces, but it is sufficient to learn basic rules of engagement, patrolling techniques, marksmanship and weapons safety, and laws. Sometimes it will be sufficient for outside parties to deploy police and army monitors to improve existing forces rather than to train new units from scratch.[16]

Compensation levels must be sufficient to minimize the risks that the force will resort to widespread extortion or take its duties less than seriously. Yet they should probably not be so high as to attract individuals for pecuniary reasons because individuals motivated in that way will generally make poor public servants.

## Law and Justice

The plight of prisoners in Rwanda, even where the ruling regime seems serious about justice and the rule of law, should remind onlookers of the critical importance of establishing acceptable and ample courts and prisons. Without them, the chances that antagonisms and hatreds will continue to simmer will be too great. It does not take many cases of injustice for already suspicious individuals to conclude that an outside force or a new indigenous government is biased and sees their people, religious group, or social class as an inherent enemy.

Proceeding quickly is important. An international mission should probably set up instruments of its own, since it may have an easier time meting out justice than would an indige-

---

16. *United Nations Peace-Keeping Information Notes*, pp. 54, 117–18; Virginia Page Fortna, "United Nations Transition Assistance Group," in Durch, ed., *The Evolution of UN Peacekeeping*, pp. 353–75.

nous group not yet trusted by much of its population. Whatever is decided about pursuing war criminals, arrests will inevitably be made for routine criminal violations, and it will be important to cultivate a reality and perception of evenhandedness vis-à-vis members of various antagonistic groups.

## Demilitarization and Economic Reconstruction

A good deal of research has been done designing the types of frugal mini-Marshall plans that war-torn developing countries might require to begin recovery. Generally, the focus of effort is in the areas of agriculture, primary education and primary health care, infrastructure, and small enterprises, and the annual price tag is on the order of several hundred million dollars per 10 million inhabitants of a country. Relief work must also continue until these development efforts have begun to produce results.[17]

In any country trying to put war behind it, it is also critical to undertake mine clearing and other efforts promptly in order to restore safety and usability to fields and roads and waterways. In addition, employment opportunities for retiring soldiers are critical if parties are to be convinced that peace is preferable to a renewal of fighting and if huge weapons stocks are to be reduced.[18] Some of these measures can be put in place in a matter of months, but economic aid will likely be needed for a number of years after the military mission has been completed.

17. See Congressional Budget Office, *Enhancing U.S. Security through Foreign Aid* (April 1994), pp. 46–47; Wolfgang H. Reinicke, "Can International Financial Institutions Prevent Internal Violence? The Sources of Ethno-National Conflict in Transitional Societies," in Abram Chayes and Antonia Handler Chayes, eds., *Preventing Conflict in the Post–Communist World* (Brookings, 1996), pp. 316–20.

18. Chester Crocker, "Afterword: Strengthening African Peacemaking and Peacekeeping," in David R. Smock, ed., *Making War and Waging Peace* (Washington, D.C.: U.S. Institute of Peace, 1993), p. 264.

A wide variety of outside and internal organizations, military and nonmilitary as well as governmental and nongovernmental alike, must coordinate their efforts. This is a challenging task, and one the international community must continue to handle better.[19]

## CONCLUSION

Beyond describing the mechanics and stages of seizing a country, it is difficult to reach systematic and general conclusions about the nature of forcible interventions. But the number of choices about basic political and security matters is limited, and there should be little confusion about what they are or about the need to make choices early in any mission.

Unfortunately, confusion has characterized a number of major operations of the 1990s. The IFOR and SFOR missions in Bosnia have labored under a paradoxical construct in which three armies have been left in one country with no plan for, much less progress toward, their reintegration—and yet with an expectation that foreign forces can leave according to a fairly firm schedule. Likewise, the intervention in Somalia was escalated to a manhunt for General Aideed without any clear understanding on the part of policymakers about the attendant risks to foreign troops and without a sustained political strategy that gave legitimacy to their actions in Somalia. Continuing to strive for a reunified Bosnia and pursuing a specific individual in Somalia are policies that can be cogently defended. But a failure to understand the risks, likely durations, and costs they entail cannot be.

19. For an important, if overstated, assessment of the challenges involved in doing so, see Michael Maren, *The Road to Hell: The Ravaging Effects of Foreign Aid and International Charity* (Free Press, 1997).

# 4
# COSTS AND CASUALTIES

W hat can one conclude about the financial costs and the likely casualties suffered by forces carrying out the operations described in chapters 2 and 3?

Determining approximate financial cost is a relatively straightforward technical matter on a per month or per year basis. Such predictions are likely to be uncertain to at least 50 percent, but that imprecision is rarely an impediment to informed decisionmaking about whether a given intervention makes sense. Missions of highly uncertain duration, by contrast, are necessarily also of highly uncertain total cost.

Although a focused military analysis can shed light on the casualty issue, it is of limited predictive value. Intangible matters—notably, the dedication and duration of indigenous resistance that outside forces encounter—are key, and they are very hard to predict. They are of two varieties: the ferocity with which indigenous forces fight on the battlefield and the determination and violence with which they may continue to resist in a guerrilla fashion even after having lost control of the country to the interveners. In the end, political judgment rather than ironclad rules of thumb will be needed to assess the likely magnitude of casualties as well as the overall desirability of attempting an intervention.[1] But general analytical frameworks of the type presented in this and preceding chapters can guide policymakers in that undertaking.

## BUDGETARY COSTS

What are the costs of intervening to restore order or to overthrow an illegitimate and brutal regime?[2] For present purposes, it is most useful to focus on the marginal or added costs of conducting the operation (taking the costs for equipping, training, and paying the units at issue as a given).

Roughly speaking, the marginal annual costs for deployment of a division-sized force tend to be $2 billion to $4 billion. That amount covers 15,000 or so combat troops plus roughly twice as many support personnel. The variability within that range is due principally to uncertainty over the amount of heavy equipment transported, the difficulty of establishing and maintaining basic support for the forces, and the movements and daily operations of the forces once they are deployed.[3] Assuming

1. Richard N. Haass, *Intervention: The Use of American Military Force in the Post–Cold War World* (Washington, D.C.: Carnegie Endowment, 1994), p. 68.

2. Determining the fixed costs of maintaining a military with enough size and structure to conduct peace operations is a more complicated, and in the end subjective, task. Uncertainty derives principally from the fact that forces can be outfitted and maintained for more than one purpose. Current U.S. military strategy and posture make no allowance for forces uniquely suited to peace operations; my own alternative described elsewhere would keep one light infantry division and part of a Marine division in the active force structure that might otherwise be retired, adding roughly $3 billion a year in costs for force structure. See Secretary of Defense Les Aspin, *Report on the Bottom-Up Review* (October 1993), pp. 22–23, 28; Michael O'Hanlon, *Defense Planning for the Late 1990s* (Brookings, 1995), pp. 34–35, 88–95.

3. The Defense Budget Project observed the convenient fact that average costs per soldier per month of deployment were about $10,000 in both the Somalia and Haiti operations. These figures translate into a total cost of about $2.5 billion for 20,000 troops over a year. See Steven Kosiak, "Potential Costs and Impact on Readiness of U.S. Peacekeeping Operations in Bosnia," Defense Budget Project, October 17, 1995, pp. 2–5.

that an intervention of the type considered would generally keep large forces deployed for one and a half to two years, in keeping with the track record in places such as Cambodia, Bosnia, and Haiti as well as the more general considerations outlined in chapter 3, total costs might be expected in most cases to range from $3 billion to $8 billion per 50,000 personnel deployed.

The uncertainty in the above range is not just a function of the location of an operation and the forces used. It is partly due to the difficulty of the calculation even after a specific mission is postulated. Indeed, the Clinton administration itself revealed just how hard it is to make accurate estimates when assessing the likely costs of deploying forces to Bosnia in late 1995. Within two months of each other in 1995, the chairman of the Joint Chiefs quoted figures of $1 billion to $1.5 billion, and the comptroller of the Department of Defense estimated $2 billion, for similar 20,000-person U.S. deployments to implement a peace accord in Bosnia.[4] (Although the Dayton accords were signed in between the publication of these two estimates, little about the nature of the anticipated U.S. participation in the operation changed as a consequence of that accord.) The estimate for the overall operation grew to nearly $2.5 billion with the submission of the Department of Defense budget request for fiscal year 1997 and later exceeded $3 billion.

A similar type of calculation can provide an algorithm for estimating the added costs of air operations. For air control operations over Iraq and Bosnia, the U.S. Air Force has recently devoted about one wing of fighter aircraft in each

4. Testimony before the House Committee on National Security and the House Committee on International Relations by Secretary of Defense William J. Perry and Chairman of the Joint Chiefs of Staff General John M. Shalikashvili, October 18, 1995; John J. Hamre, Under Secretary of Defense, Comptroller, "Bosnia Peace Implementation Force," December 1, 1995.

theater at an annual cost of about $200 million per operation. (Any costs from lost aircraft are additional.)[5]

Overall costs can, if one wishes greater detail or precision, be broken down into three categories: transport, operations and support, and replacement of equipment. For each, the Gulf War experience provides the most ready source of data. Compared with other locations, it may underestimate costs in logistics and in support, given that Saudi infrastructure is considerably better than one could expect to find in most other developing countries (particularly for wartime conditions). But it may overestimate costs associated with transport and with operations, given the quantity of heavy and high-technology equipment that was deployed to that conflict as well as the tempo at which it was operated.

For the one-way transportation of about half a million personnel and their associated equipment, much of it heavy ground equipment, the Department of Defense required about $3.5 billion. Roughly one-third of those costs were for airlift, nearly evenly distributed among the three military departments of Army, Navy, and Air Force; two-thirds were in sealift, almost exactly split between the Army and the Navy with only $100 million or so attributable to the Air Force.

Scaling down by a factor of ten, for a smaller operation of the type considered in this study, one could estimate round-trip transportation costs as about $500 million to $1 billion. For light forces easily transportable by air, the total might be less (but not necessarily a great deal less, given the need both to deploy those forces and to sustain them with supplies over an extended period).[6] Given the military's preference to rotate troops and

5. Secretary of Defense William J. Perry, *Annual Report to the President and the Congress* (February 1995), pp. 39, 40, 205; General Accounting Office, *Peace Operations: Estimated Fiscal Year 1995 Costs to the United States*, GAO/NSIAD-95-138BR (May 1995), p. 18; data provided by the U.S. Air Force, March 1996.

6. Congressional Budget Office, "Costs of Operation Desert Shield," January 1991, p. 4; Office of Management and Budget, "United States Costs in the Persian Gulf Conflict and Foreign Contributions to Offset Such Costs," April 27, 1991, pp. 3–5.

often equipment after a year even if a mission continues thereafter, this number is also reasonable as an annualized cost estimate for deployments lasting longer than twelve months.

Operations and support costs are usually divided into two subcategories: personnel on the one hand, and operations and maintenance on the other. The personnel costs are the smaller of the two. They could include added hostile-fire pay of roughly $1,500 a year per soldier, totaling about $75 million over a year for a deployment of 50,000 U.S. troops. Added costs for callups of reserve units could push the overall total for personnel to more than $100 million.[7]

For operations and maintenance (O&M), costs in the Gulf War were about $11 billion for the six-month period through the end of February. Nearly three-quarters or about $7.5 billion was for Army forces, $1.7 billion for the Navy including the Marines, and $1.2 billion for the Air Force. The O&M category includes costs for fuel, military construction, equipment maintenance and repair, spare parts, and various other types of support including provision of health care, food, and water.

To use these figures as a basis for estimating the costs of an infantry-oriented intervention may overstate things. However, the added annual operating costs associated with the tempo of the Vietnam War (above and beyond those that would be expected simply because the U.S. military was larger during the Vietnam period) were also large, approaching $10 billion in the peak years of effort for a half-million person deployment. That equals roughly $1 billion a year for every 50,000 people (1996 dollars).

Added costs could arise from replacing any equipment destroyed or expended. This procurement category can include combat weapons systems such as helicopters, ordnance, and support vehicles. It is difficult to estimate associated costs. But consistent with the estimate that intervening forces could suffer

7. CBO, "Costs of Operation Desert Shield," p. 17; OMB, "United States Costs in the Persian Gulf Conflict," p. 7.

hundreds of casualties might be losses of perhaps ten heli-copters and ten larger armored vehicles as well as a greater number of jeeps and trucks. Factoring in again as much money for replacement of expended ammunition, several hundreds of millions of dollars might be required to restore equipment stocks to their pre-intervention levels.[8]

In all, for 50,000 troops, a billion dollars might be spent on transport, at least a billion a year in operations in theater, and several hundred million more on replacement of equipment as well as on personnel and medical costs and the like. These numbers could, however, vary by at least 50 percent in either direction in practice. Given a certain size force with a certain complement of equipment, the bulk of these costs would be independent of how much if any combat it engaged in.

It is not within the scope of this study to provide equal detail on the non-DOD costs associated with intensive peace opera-tions or interventions to restore order. But the U.S. share of those costs—for humanitarian relief, refugee care, police and court assistance, and reconstruction—tends in the aggregate to be roughly comparable to military costs if experience to date is a reliable guide. For example, the General Accounting Office estimated that the United States spent $3.7 billion in fiscal year 1995 on peace operations broadly defined, with $1.8 billion incurred by DOD and $1.9 billion by other federal agen-cies. The latter costs were in turn split between U.S. support for UN peacekeeping, funding for other countries' participation in peace operations, and strictly nonmilitary efforts.

## CASUALTY ESTIMATES

How many casualties and deaths might outside troops be expected to suffer during an operation to restore order? Given

---

8. OMB, "United States Costs in the Persian Gulf Conflict," p. 10.

the political and military variables at play, a formula or algorithm for calculating casualties is elusive. But data from several relevant military operations in the past, from various training exercises, and from other guides provide a number of benchmarks.

Casualties could be incurred in perhaps three main ways during this type of operation. First, particularly in the absence of consent from indigenous armed groups, they could result from the initial deployment to establish a lodgment and then during the deployment of forces throughout the territory of the country at issue. Even if a cease-fire was in hand, troops would be vulnerable to accidents—given the number of aircraft and helicopter operations that would be going on and the number of roads and bridges that would be used by heavy vehicles for perhaps the first time in quite a while.

Second, intervening forces could be vulnerable to counterattack. It could occur on a battlefield scale, but it would more likely take the form of guerrilla resistance and terrorism as well as mines. The extent of such opposition would vary greatly from situation to situation, ranging from quite minor to very significant.

Finally, troops would suffer casualties in any firefights they initiated to weaken a given armed group or capture its leaders. This last source of casualties would be in large part a function of the mission's exit strategy and other specific characteristics. Interveners could, for example, elect not to pursue war criminals, powerful military leaders, and certain armies. Avoiding such confrontations may keep outside troops' casualties down—though it may also impede long-term political reconciliation in the country at issue. Tradeoffs are involved.

To get a sense of the numbers of casualties that might be suffered, consider first a different type of battle—the war in the Persian Gulf. In the course of Desert Shield and Desert Storm, almost 400 Americans died. Of those, 150 were directly killed by the Iraqis; almost 100 were lost in training and related activities before the war even began; and another 150 died from encountering unexploded ordnance, accidental fire from their compatriots, or other "nonhostile" acts during the war.[9]

Thus, using combined air-armor warfare, the U.S.-led coalition achieved a highly favorable "casualty exchange ratio:" it killed or wounded at least ten Iraqis for every one of its own soldiers hurt over the course of the entire operation. Indeed, it may have approached a ratio as high as 100:1, though the absence of precise data on Iraqi casualties makes a definitive calculation impossible.[10] If one could simply scale the data from the Gulf War to an operation roughly one-tenth the size, as might be expected in a forcible humanitarian intervention, the multilateral force might be expected to lose on the order of 20 to 30 individuals killed over several months of operations. (Another 75 to 150 might be wounded, if typical ratios of killed to wounded from recent wars apply—though the ratio might be somewhat different for noncombat accidents.)

Of course, restoring order in civil conflicts or overthrowing brutal regimes perpetrating horrors on their citizens would generally be a much different type of operation than Desert Storm. U.S. and western advantages in the infantry combat that might be expected would still be substantial. But in all likelihood, they would not be as great as in the Gulf War.[11]

The Desert Shield/Storm experience does, however, highlight the fact that intensive military operations tend to cause casu-

9. Department of Defense, *Defense Almanac 96* (Alexandria, Va.: American Forces Information Service, 1996), p. 44.

10. John Mueller, "The Perfect Enemy: Assessing the Gulf War," *Security Studies*, vol. 5, no. 1 (Autumn 1995), p. 96; Robert L. Goldrich, "Casualties and Maximum Number of Troops Deployed in Recent U.S. Military Ground Combat Actions," Congressional Research Service, October 8, 1993.

11. That is not merely a function of the nature of the warfare at issue, but also of Iraqi incompetence in the Gulf War. For a penetrating analysis of this issue, see Stephen Biddle, "Victory Misunderstood: What the Gulf War Tells Us About the Future of Conflict," *International Security*, vol. 21, no. 2 (Fall 1996), pp. 139–79.

alties even when there is no shooting. Even in peacetime, the U.S. military generally loses tens of aircraft a year in serious accidents, of which a number involve fatalities. Most are with only one or a small number of crewman aboard, but AWACS aircraft and transport helicopters and planes also crash. The Army, for example, plans on 0.3 percent attrition per year in its helicopter fleet. Of its fleet of 8,000 aircraft, anywhere from 100 to 500 might be associated with a single division—meaning that one or two would probably be lost in a given year even during peacetime.[12] Similarly, vehicles also are involved in accidents. Overall, well over 100 U.S. military personnel die each year in training and other routine activities.[13] For a military operation involving a ground division, an Air Force wing or two, and a Navy ship squadron or task force, roughly one-tenth to one-twentieth of the U.S. military force structure would be involved. Over a year's time frame, therefore, perhaps ten deaths and a total of fifty casualties might be expected—even if the mission was no more dangerous than routine training and standard operations.

The experiences from several other recent U.S. military operations also underscore the risks of death from accident, mines, and the like. In the Iranian hostage rescue mission of 1980, all eight U.S. deaths were due to "nonhostile" causes. In Lebanon, Grenada, and Panama, a total of ten troops lost their lives from such causes (the remaining 295 were killed by adversarial action, most in the tragic bombing of the Marine barracks in Lebanon). In Somalia, fourteen out of forty-three U.S. deaths were caused by nonhostile events. In Haiti, no hostile-fire deaths but four U.S. losses overall were reported; a similar experience appears to be unfolding in Bosnia.[14]

12. Congressional Budget Office, *An Analysis of U.S. Army Helicopter Programs* (December 1995), pp. 7, 24–25.
13. U.S. Air Force Flight Safety Division; Naval Safety Center; Army Safety Center.
14. *Defense Almanac 96*, p. 44.

But in general, even interventions low on combat should probably be expected to be more dangerous than peacetime training. Simply operating in a foreign and, in all likelihood, land mine-strewn area would make things somewhat more dangerous. Unlike operations in the Gulf, moreover, most countries would not provide the quality of infrastructure (and weather) that Saudi Arabia lent coalition forces.

In the case of the former Yugoslavia, for example, a UN operation averaging some 30,000 well-trained soldiers lost a considerable number of individuals. Slightly more than 200 were killed and more than 1,500 suffered injuries in about three years of operations. Those rather high casualty rates were the result of land mines and accidents and of sniping and other hostile fire. This rate is roughly 2 percent a year, several times greater than the annualized rate associated with peacetime operations or Desert Storm.[15] Although UNPROFOR did not involve U.S. soldiers, they too would be vulnerable to such threats as land mines, even when riding in modern U.S. vehicles.[16]

For protracted infantry combat, casualties could be higher still. Even lightly-armed and loosely organized forces would have certain advantages when fighting on their home soil.[17] For example, in U.S. Army exercises that mimic real warfare, minimally armed U.S. units who are home-based at Ft. Polk Louisiana's Joint Readiness Training Center and accustomed to its terrain generally extract at least as many "casualties" as

15. United Nations, *United Nations Peacekeeping Information Notes*, December 1994 and December 1995.

16. The Army concurs. See Center for Army Lessons Learned, "Handbook for the Soldier in Operations other than War," Handbook 94-4, Fort Leavenworth, Kansas, July 1994, pp. II-9 through II-10.

17. Sun Tzu, *The Art of War* (London: Oxford University Press, 1963), pp. 66–70; B. H. Liddell Hart, *Strategy* (London: Faber and Faber, Ltd., 1967), pp. 334–37; U.S. Marine Corps, *Tactics* (June 1991); U.S. Army, *Field Manual 100-5: Operations* (June 1993), pp. 7-1 through 7-3.

they suffer from normal U.S. infantry forces deployed there temporarily for exercises.

Fortunately, most militias overseas are not as competent as the "opposition" forces stationed at Ft. Polk. They may figure out how to use terrain to their advantage and use speed and coordinated movements as well. But most would not train in combined-arms operations or be proficient in staggering their movements, using smoke for cover properly, digging in correctly, or using anti-aircraft weapons effectively. Intervening forces would also possess advantages resulting from their weaponry and their other equipment such as night vision optics, advanced communications gear, counterartillery radars, and helicopters.[18]

On balance, were intervening forces fortunate, their advantages might translate into casualty exchange ratios around 10:1 in their favor during infantry battles. At a minimum, as official military documents indicate, a U.S. or NATO force would expect to extract a 3:1 exchange ratio against an enemy infantry force and could in fact probably achieve at least that.[19] (If coping with a well-orchestrated terrorist campaign, they might make out less favorably in proportional terms—but then the scale of violence would probably be limited too.)

What do these exchange ratios imply about total expected casualties? Most armed groups in civil conflicts number in the thousands or tens of thousands at most. An extraordinarily dedicated group might fight until it had only a small fraction of its initial strength; most would probably not accept that level of punishment unless casualties were suffered gradually enough

18. U.S. Army, *Field Manual 100-23: Peace Operations* (December 1994), pp. 36–44.

19. On Somalia, see Terrence Lyons and Ahmed I. Samatar, *Somalia* (Brookings, 1995), p. 59; and "U.S. Military Operations in Somalia," Hearings before the U.S. Senate Committee on Armed Services, S. Hrg. 103-846, pp. 62–63. See also U.S. Army, *Ranger Handbook* (Fort Benning, Georgia: Ranger Training Brigade, U.S. Army Infantry School, July 1992), pp. 5-20 through 5-41.

that recruitment of new soldiers could replenish the ranks. By this line of argument, intervening forces might be expected to suffer wounded and killed ranging roughly from tens to many hundreds of their soldiers, and perhaps over a thousand, in the course of intensive infantry combat operations. The range of uncertainty depends somewhat on the armaments of indigenous resistance forces, but even more on their level of military competence and their willingness to risk death.[20]

Another way to think of these numbers that may make them seem more real is to consider when and where outside forces might suffer casualties. In their deployment stage, aircraft could be vulnerable to surface-to-air missiles, rocket-propelled grenades, and small-arms fire, and bases could be vulnerable to sabotage. But the second stage would probably be even more dangerous, since it would require forces to disperse, traveling via roads they did not know well or flying aircraft into urban areas that militias could use as camouflage to launch attacks. Ambushes of convoys and newly established bases would also be among the greatest risks. The third phase, that of direct combat operations, could be more dangerous still—whether the operation was an opposed intervention from the start or an effort to reimpose a cease-fire that domestic parties had originally accepted. The patrols and other security operations that would be part of the force's daily routine by that point could also be hazardous due to sniping, ambush, and booby-trap explosives.

What numbers of casualties might be expected in each of these tactical settings? It is of course difficult to generalize, but some observations are possible (and one specific example, that of U.S. forces in Mogadishu in October, 1993, is discussed in more detail below).

20. For a similar conclusion about the specific case of Bosnia, see Michael E. Brown, "Operation Balkan Storm," *Washington Post*, July 25, 1995, p. A15; for a very good analysis about the role of military competence in Vietnam, see Neil Sheehan, *A Bright Shining Lie* (New York: Random House, 1988), pp. 201–65.

Assuming that proper security procedures of the type discussed in chapter 2 are scrupulously followed during the initial deployment phase and no large aircraft are shot down, most tactical engagements would tend to involve vehicles containing only a few individuals. The occasional ambush might be successful enough, even against top-of-the-line forces, to destroy the lead vehicle in a convoy; the well-disguised and well-aimed surface-to-air missile, or perhaps even a rocket-propelled grenade, might down an occasional helicopter.

Attacks of the above variety might occur only every few days or weeks, succeeding some of the time. Sniping and the threat of land mines would be more omnipresent, but they would generally put fewer people at risk at a time. All told, one or several soldiers might become casualties on a typical day, and groups might be injured or killed every few days or weeks, while the three main steps of the deployment were being executed.

As sobering as it may be to confront the fact, therefore, the results of U.S. military operations in Somalia in 1993 should not be viewed as particularly unusual or poor. There were probably no simple tactical adjustments that would have prevented substantial losses, given the basic nature of the operation (in contrast, for example, to the tragedy in Lebanon a decade earlier, when nearly 250 Marines lost their lives in a bombing of their insufficiently protected barracks).[21] Even in the ill-fated firefight in Mogadishu on October 3, 1993, in which eighteen Americans died and about eighty-five were wounded, U.S. forces reportedly suffered only one-tenth the casualties incurred by Somalis, and about one-fifteenth their number of deaths. U.S. forces had better body armor and

21. For an indication of the seriousness with which the U.S. military has taken measures to avoid vulnerability of its bases in the wake of the 1983 bombings of the Marine barracks in Beirut, see Center for Army Lessons Learned, "Handbook for the Soldier in Operations other than War (OOTW)," Handbook no. 94-4, Fort Leavenworth, Kansas, July 1994, p. II-11.

medical treatment, making for a lower ratio of dead to wounded than for the Somalis.

Had the Ranger reaction force or the backup Quick Reaction Force of the 10th Mountain Division been given more armored vehicles by leaders in Washington, as had been requested by Major General Thomas Montgomery, the top-ranking U.S. officer in Somalia at the time, U.S. deaths might have been fewer. But they still would have probably included more than fifteen soldiers killed, according to the judgments of commanders from that operation as reflected in later Senate testimony. General principles of infantry combat, some of which were discussed in chapter 2, tend to support their judgment. Had further operations been conducted against the Aideed forces left reeling by the October 3 firefight, exchange ratios even more favorable to the U.S. side might have been achieved (for example, by flying helicopters out of the range of rocket-propelled grenades, even at the cost of reduced accuracy of helicopter fire). But additional U.S. losses would have been nearly inevitable, probably totaling more than a few individuals.[22]

Still, the Somalia case was a relatively difficult one given the dedication and resolve of indigenous forces. The recent invasions of Panama and Grenada provide useful indicators at the easier end of the spectrum. The United States lost 23 and 19 soldiers, with an additional 324 and 115 wounded, respectively, in those operations, in which acute phases lasted roughly three to four days. The Panama operation encountered some 5,000 opposition forces, the Grenada mission about 1,000.[23]

22. The addition of more AC-130 gunships, by contrast, would probably not have made a substantial difference in the operation because overhead reconnaissance and firepower capabilities were provided by other aircraft in ways that U.S. commanders found quite adequate. See "U.S. Military Operations in Somalia," Hearings before the U.S. Senate Committee on Armed Services, S. Hrg. 103-846, May 12, 1994, pp. 8–11, 29–33, 35, 45, 49–53, 62–63.

23. Goldrich, "Casualties"; Trevor N. Dupuy, *International Military and Defense Encyclopedia* (Washington, D. C.: Brassey's, 1993), pp. 1091–93, 2099–2101.

It might also be noted that in the Panama invasion, the actual capture of General Noriega was not a significant determinant of U.S. casualties. Seizing the country's major infrastructure and defeating its armed forces is what caused U.S. soldiers to lose their lives. Clearly, the expulsion of the Haitian military junta during the initial stage of the U.S. military deployment to that country was a successful and low-cost use of force to change fundamentally the basic structure of power within the country at issue. By contrast, roughly half of the twenty-nine U.S. soldiers who were killed by hostile action in Somalia lost their lives directly in the pursuit of General Aideed.[24]

These examples underscore the difficulty of predicting how much the pursuit of war criminals or other individuals, or attempts to weaken specific armed factions, will determine casualties in a given situation. It is very hard to generalize.

The Panama case in particular indicates why the U.S. military prefers to use simultaneous, rapid, and concentrated attacks against an enemy—not simply to have a safety margin, or to send an intimidating political message, but because such attacks tend to break down the opponent's physical ability to resist and to organize counterattacks. They should thus tend to precipitate capitulation. Limiting the duration and scope of combat in this way is in the end the best means of keeping casualties to a minimum.[25] In the specific case of Panama, the casualty exchange ratio was not extremely lopsided in the U.S. favor—only about sixty-five to seventy Panamanian soldiers died in the fighting. But at least 1,500 surrendered; it was due

24. Department of Defense, *Defense Almanac 96* (Alexandria, Va.: American Forces Information Service, 1996), p. 44.

25. *Field Manual 100-5*, pp. 3-11, 7-0, 7-3; *FMFM 1-3: Tactics*, pp. 42-59. As Trevor Dupuy has shown by quantitative analysis of a wide range of conflicts, even superior and successful militaries generally suffer daily casualty rates on the order of 1 percent of those forces directly engaged in battle. See Trevor N. Dupuy, *Attrition: Forecasting Battle Casualties and Equipment Losses in Modern War* (Fairfax, Va.: HERO Books, 1990), pp. 106–07, 139.

to that latter number, and the associated quickness of the victory, that the U.S. military operation was overwhelming and had such a low casualty rate.[26] Future operations should aspire to a similar outcome.

Clearly, in many cases it is not just the style of the intervention, but the political goals it is seen as serving that will determine the extent of resistance and thus the casualties. For example, an intervention to push back the Bosnian Serbs—in the sense of driving them back from the 70 percent of territory they held to the 50 percent that was deemed practical under the Vance-Owen and contact group frameworks—might have been achievable at modest cost in 1994 or 1995. The Croatian army, fighting in conjunction with Bosnian Croats and Muslims in some cases, demonstrated in the late summer of 1995 how feasible it was to conduct a "Balkan blitzkrieg" at low cost provided that the adversary could be presented with a reasonable alternative to fighting to the death. In those operations in Croatia and western Bosnia, local Serbs were quickly either defeated or intimidated into withdrawing, largely because they were not required to relinquish all of their strategic goals, but only specific pieces of relatively marginal territory.[27]

26. See Hearing before the House Armed Services Committee, July 7, 1992, "The Invasion of Panama: How Many Innocent Bystanders Perished?," 102 Cong., 2 Sess., Committee Print no. 11 (Washington, D.C.: Government Printing Office, 1992), p. 2; Joint Hearings before the Senate Armed Services Committee and Select Committee on Intelligence, October 6 and 17 and December 22, 1989, "1989 Events in Panama," Senate Hearing 101-881 (Washington, D.C.: Government Printing Office, 1990), p. 133.

27. Michael Brown of Harvard University had predicted a similar outcome a few weeks earlier, for an operation conducted by outside forces. He felt that the operation would go quickly and result in no more than 1,000 western deaths if its mandate was limited to pushing the Serbs back from some of the land they then held and effecting a partition of the country. See Michael E. Brown, "Operation Balkan Storm," *Washington Post*, July 25, 1995, p. 15.

Although infantry combat has been of critical importance in Bosnia, armor and maneuver have been too. For example, in the Bosnian Serb army's capture of Sre-

Many observers argue that in places such as Panama and Iraq, opposition forces "did not really fight," making U.S. victories in those places less than impressive. Those observers are in some ways missing the point. As Sun Tzu discerned millennia ago and as the Rwandan Patriotic Front demonstrated in overthrowing the Hutu genocidaires in 1994, the best military victories are those that do not have to be slugged out on the battlefield, but can be obtained by the rapid surrender of an enemy that quickly recognizes itself outpositioned or outmatched and decides on an alternative to fighting to the death. Pursuing this type of victory is in the end usually the only reliable way to fight a low-casualty war.

All told, these latter examples confirm the estimates made earlier: that an intervening force of roughly 50,000 individuals would likely incur somewhere between tens and many hundreds of casualties in an operation lasting on the order of a year. Deaths would probably be about one-fifth of the total, or anywhere from roughly 10 to well over 100. Unless poorly conceived or executed, or unless attempted in a country where extensive guerrilla combat ensued, outside forces would almost certainly not suffer casualties approaching or exceeding 1,000 in a year for interventions against relatively weak opponents of the type considered here.

## CONCLUSION

If outside powers choose carefully where to intervene and employ a significant number of combat troops from the United

---

brenica in July of 1995, they were outnumbered by Bosnian government forces, roughly by a 3,000 to 2,000 margin, but possessed superiority in heavy weaponry: 20 to 50 artillery pieces versus 0 for the Bosnian government, and up to 10 tanks versus 0 for the Bosnian government. Western forces would have been able to muster similarly overwhelming advantages against the Serbs. See News Briefing, Office of the Assistant Secretary of Defense for Public Affairs, July 11, 1995, p. 8.

States or a small handful of other countries with top-notch militaries, they can rapidly restore security in small and medium-sized countries beset by widespread violence. They will suffer losses, and their operations will typically cost from $1 billion to several billion dollars annually for missions generally lasting at least eighteen months to two years. They will themselves cause losses to armed individuals and perhaps some innocent civilians from the country at issue. But the job they will need to do is fairly clear, and they will be capable of performing it.

Selective humanitarian interventions can often do a great deal to mitigate human suffering and to reduce the prevalence of conflict around the world at modest financial and human cost to intervening countries. The militaries of the United States and several other countries can lead them successfully. The onus is on political leaders to have the courage to undertake such operations when they can save tens of thousands of lives at modest risk and cost—but to have the wisdom and discretion to avoid them or rethink them when their prospects look poor.

Policymakers' judgments on whether and how to intervene should be informed by military analysis of the type appearing in this study. For example, they should understand the relationship between the size of a country and the number of forces likely to be needed to establish order throughout it, as well as the relationships between the country's geography on the one hand and logistics and lift requirements on the other. When considering involvement in civil wars characterized by reasonably well-armed and disciplined fighters, they should often be prepared for their own troops to suffer hundreds of casualties. They should also recognize that manhunts are inherently difficult, that trying to "disarm factions" is dangerous for similar reasons—and yet that leaving hostile armies or extremist leaders in place on disputed territory will generally impede development of a sound exit strategy that can be set to even a rough schedule.

Decisions to intervene will and should also be influenced by domestic politics in countries like the United States that might do the intervening. As noted, these types of operations are difficult to get right, and they demand considerable time and attention from top-level officials in countries sending troops. That limits the number that can be done properly in any given span of time. Also, such missions require certain types of military capabilities, such as strategic transport, that may be in short supply at any given moment.

Any decision to conduct a forcible humanitarian intervention should also be heavily influenced by the politics of the country at issue. Notably, it should hinge largely on an assessment of the goals, commitment, competence, and domestic appeal of significant armed groups within the country at issue. These factors will have much to say about the potential that outside forces will encounter fierce and protracted guerrilla resistance of a type that would usually make intervention undesirable. Policymakers should also take note of the prospects that a more stable political landscape can be cobbled together in the course of a mission. Finally, they should take account of the scale of suffering that would result without the intervention, compared with that likely to result (immediately and over time) if outside forces do deploy.

Among other things, these considerations argue in favor of two interventions that were not conducted: a mission to prevent genocide in Rwanda in 1994 and also a deployment to stop civil war in Liberia in the early 1990s (though not to restore control of the country to the corrupt president, Samuel Doe). They also support the U.S.-led interventions that were undertaken to overthrow the Haitian junta and to feed starving Somalis. But in the latter case, military and political considerations argue strongly that pursuing Aideed without an explicit change of mission and without recognizing the high risks of casualties was wrong.

Bosnia presents the most complicated recent case. There, an early intervention to reunify the country under Muslim government rule would likely have precipitated a severe Serb counterreaction against outside forces and thus been unwise. But a more limited operation to prevent the worse genocidal atrocities and to drive back Serbs from some of the land they held would have been justified and probably workable much earlier than when it was finally carried out (by the Croat-led ground offensive at least as much as by western airpower).

As for the future in Bosnia, two elements of western policy seem highly questionable on military grounds. First, allowing three generally hostile armies to coexist within one contested territory does not bode well for the country's future and does not appear consistent with a sound exit strategy. Facing up to the apparent inevitability of partition seems a wiser course unless outside forces are prepared to remain in significant numbers for many years. Second, pursuing war criminals with armed forces or resettling refugees in their original homes in a forcible reversal of ethnic cleansing would amount to a fundamental redefinition of the military mission. Without a full-fledged congressional and NATO-wide debate to do so, that would be an unwise policy.

Military analysis cannot resolve fundamentally political questions, but it can reveal logically inconsistent and unworkable approaches to selective humanitarian intervention. Flawed approaches, regrettably enough, remain common. But so does the imperative for action in many destructive wars around the world.

# Index

Accidents. *See* Casualties
Afghanistan, 30, 37, 44, 51
Africa, 49, 56
Aideed, Mohammed: casualties and risks, 14, 61; future role of, 49; pursuit of, 14-15, 34, 39, 53, 80. *See also* Somalia
Airborne Division, 82d, 20
Aircraft: airlifts, 21-23, 29-30, 31, 65; casualties, 70, 73, 74; civilian, 21n4; cost of air operations, 64-65, 66; helicopters, 35, 36; gunships, 35, 39, 75n22
Airlines, commercial, 22
Algeria, 44
Amin, Idi, 34, 49, 54
Angola, 6, 18, 32
Armored Division, 1st, 29
Arusha peace accord, 18.

Bakuramutsa, Manzi, 3n4
Bangladesh, 52
Bosnia: casualties, 70, 77; costs of, 64-65; Dayton accords, 15, 64; division of, 16; intervention in, 1, 15, 16, 81; military forces, 24, 61, 77n27; political issues, 15; state/nation-building, 48, 56; Vance-Owen framework, 77; war criminals, 54
Brazil, 52
Britain, 11-12, 43
Brown, Michael, 77n27

Cambodia, 48
Casualties: accidents, 31, 68, 71; counterattack, 68; infantry combat, 71-72, 73, 74; in interventions, 12, 13-14, 16, 35, 52, 66-67, 69-70, 79; mines, 35n26, 60, 71, 74; peacetime, 70, 71-72; Persian Gulf War, 68-69; political issues and, 77; public opinion of, 3; total expected, 72-73, 76n25, 78; when and where suffered, 73-74
Chechnya, 50
Chile, 49
China, 48, 52